PLANT CLOSINGS

PLANT CLOSINGS

Power, Politics, and Workers

LAWRENCE E. ROTHSTEIN
University of Rhode Island

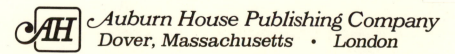
Auburn House Publishing Company
Dover, Massachusetts • London

Library of Congress Cataloging in Publication Data

Rothstein, Lawrence E.
  Plant closings.

  Includes index.
  1. Plant shutdowns—United States.   2 Plant
shutdowns—France.   I. Title.
HD5708.55.U6R68   1986   338.6′042   85–23025
ISBN 0–86569–121–5

Printed in the United States of America

FOREWORD

During an extended period of residence in Europe in the 1970's, I was reminded daily by the media of worker and community concern in France over then-current plant closings and employee layoffs. Militant worker reaction to threatened shutdowns had its most extreme form in the highly publicized occupation and running of the LIP watch plant in France by workers in 1974. But worker demands were also widespread for more extensive national legislation requiring prior notice to workers and communities of plant shutdowns, worker participation in decisions concerning industrial policies leading to shutdowns, and benefits for workers laid off for economic reasons. The adoption of such legislation has been a common response in Europe to widespread layoffs.

The adoption of plant closing legislation to offset the detrimental effects on communities and workers thus appeared to this American living in Europe to be a normal response to a serious human problem. Returning to the United States in the late seventies, in the midst of an economic recession in the Northeast industrialized regions, I found plant closings once again in the news, with plant closing legislation proposed as one response. But plant closing legislation has generally been unsuccessful in the United States. Efforts to adopt federal legislation recently failed, and few states or local communities have adopted such laws. Why, I asked myself, was a response so widely adopted in European countries so unsuccessful in the United States? Professor Rothstein's book has provided a thoughtful answer to my query.

This book on plant closings is a sophisticated and well-documented analysis of the differing political, legal, and social climates in the United States and France which have led, respectively, to failure to adopt plant closing legislation in the United States but to successful adoption in France. Professor Rothstein's

v

experience has been the converse of mine: Observing the failure to adopt plant closing legislation in the United States, he was led to study the French experience. In addition to his scholarly study of the U.S. labor movement, Rothstein was actively involved in promoting the adoption of plant closing legislation in Rhode Island—an effort which, like many others in the United States, eventually proved unsuccessful. A year of research in France provided him with insights concerning the U.S. labor movement and the lack of U.S. worker militancy in fighting plant shutdowns.

This book is clearly of interest to students of comparative labor relations, but it should also be of great interest to all who are concerned with U.S. industrial problems. Professor Rothstein lays the responsibility for the failure of plant closing legislation in the United States to what he characterizes as three myths—about big labor, the business climate, and legality. He refers to these myths as "widely accepted analyses, conceptions, and perceptions with ambiguous or illusory factual support." They provide the basis for a thoughtful theoretical analysis of the detailed factual material Professor Rothstein amassed on plant closings in France and the United States.

Not limiting himself to theoretical analysis, Rothstein offers concrete suggestions to the U.S. labor movement on overcoming the present decline of trade unionism and on improving the promotion of workers' interests. This book highlights the differing historical and ideological backgrounds of European and American labor movements, and it will encourage the reader to further reflection and comparative study. By focussing on this crucial worker concern, Rothstein has provided a fresh perspective on current U.S. labor problems.

VIRGINIA A. LEARY
Professor, Faculty of Law and Jurisprudence
State University of New York at Buffalo

PREFACE

It has been my good fortune to have had the chance to research and write this book. My interests and passions were united in the project. As a political theorist, I have had a long-time interest in democracy and the structure of power relations. As a legal services attorney, I have had an intimate acquaintance with legal mythology and its effects on those struggling for some power over their lives.

In 1979, a number of plant closings in Rhode Island led to the formation of the Community Labor Organizing Committee (CLOC) (now the Community Labor Coalition) by militant trade unionists and community activists. They were seeking a more active response than offered by their unions or social service agencies to the problems of laid-off and threatened workers. As one element of their program, they proposed plant closing legislation. To bring together interested people and public officials, CLOC sponsored a conference on runaway shops. The speakers were both moving and informative. (Some of these statements are quoted in Chapter 2.) I was impressed by the effort CLOC had mounted and by the dedicated and intelligent people I met at that conference. I joined CLOC and assisted in the drafting and advocacy of several plant closing bills.

By gathering data to support the bills and discussing the bills with the less committed, I soon found that a major obstacle facing their passage was a widely accepted mythology that is easily refuted by available data and yet firmly entrenched even among trade unionists. The campaign for plant closing legislation led me to the questions I ask in the first chapter concerning the existence and effects of this mythology.

Those questions could only be partially answered by investigating the American experience. I soon discovered it was necessary to compare what I had seen in the United States with labor politics in another country. The recent militancy of the French labor movement, especially in Longwy, and the existence of a comprehensive administrative procedure for authorizing (or rejecting) economic layoffs drew my attention to France.

I arrived in France while the election victory of Mitterrand and the coalition of left-wing parties was still being toasted with champagne, and I left as the disillusionment was setting in. While there, observations, interviews, and documents enabled me to delve deeply into the workings of the French administrative procedures for authorizing economic layoffs and into the labor movement's responses to plant closings and layoffs. Moreover, I was able to get a feeling for how the change in political atmosphere affected the treatment of plant closings.

After considering the evidence that is presented in this book, I was convinced that militant workers gain more than quiescent ones and that, particularly in the United States, militancy has been suppressed as much by a business mythology as by the naked use of power.

The more I analyzed the information I was uncovering in comparing the plight of French and American workers facing plant closings and layoffs, the more I wondered whether there was something going on other than a simple economic readjustment to a period of low growth. Were plant closings and layoffs merely efforts by business to share the economic burdens of competition and slipping demand with workers? The answer appeared to me to be "No."

The data seemed to reveal the unity of government and business and a pervasive mythology that augmented their power. A new corporatism (variants of which formed the economic base for Fascism in Italy and Naziism in Germany) was being forged that was inimical to the notion of popular sovereignty central to democracy. Major political decisions were being labeled "private" or "business" decisions and handed over to "experts" who discussed and resolved them in secrecy. The public and, most especially workers, were barred from participating in the decision making. The resulting decisions, generally detrimental to the interests of workers, were called "technical," "necessary," or "inevitable" and accompanied by a brief mention of the "business climate," "foreign competition," or the "balance of payments."

The one thing they were never called by the decision makers was "political."

The only possible counter to this development was for militant workers allied with other dynamic, progressive movements to confront this corporatism and its business mythology. Worker militancy, however, requires some institutional and community support. The recommendations made at the end of Chapter 2 and reviewed in successive chapters are aimed at creating this support. These recommendations may seem a great leap from the analysis of plant closings and the responses to them. You, the reader, must judge whether the leap is justified.

ACKNOWLEDGMENTS

I would like to thank first Yvonne Teyber and Sharon Wood-mansee without whose typing and editorial assistance very little could have been accomplished. John Coen, John "Spider" Burbank, Al Martin, George Nee, and George Sweeting of the Community Labor Organizing Committee (now Community Labor Coalition) deserve thanks for getting me involved in plant closing research and for their aid and encouragement.

Initial French contacts made through Joel Dirlam, Professor Emeritus of Economics of the University of Rhode Island, and a subsequent, joint grant from the National Science Foundation and the Centre National de Recherches Scientifiques Exchange of Scientists enabled me to spend my sabbatical year in France doing research. My colleagues, Al Killilea, Tim Hennessey, Ed Leduc, and Ted Schmidt, aided me greatly in applying for this grant. My wife, Bobbi Rothstein, encouraged me, accompanied me, listened to me, and often corrected me in the research and writing of this book. My friends, the Boulles, kindly assured that I missed nothing of French culture, cuisine and wine while I worked.

I wish to thank Alain d'Iribarne, Jean-Jacques Silvestre, Anne Durand-Rival, François Eyraud, Roger Cornu, Gerald Dubray and Frédérique Rychener of the Laboratoire de l'Economie et de la Sociologie du Travail (LEST) for their support, ideas, and contacts. LEST was the base of operations during most of my stay in France. I am grateful to everyone there for their assistance and patience.

For their ideas, trade union and government contacts, and encouragement, thanks also go to Jacques Garnier of the Institut Régional de Travail, Olivier Kourchid of the Groupe de Sociologie du Travail, Hugues Puel and Anne Mayère of the Institute

Economie et Humanisme, and François Michon of the Seminaire d'Economie de Travail. I am happy to say that I thank all those mentioned above, not only for their assistance with my work, but also for their friendship.

I was able to interview many trade unionists and labor inspectors. Among them I wish to thank especially Marie-France Derrien, M. Charriaux, Christian Viel, Gilbert Dupin, Pierre Massabau, Michel Potoudis, Francis Bertin, Mario Tessarotto, Massimo Trinoli, and Christiane Ulrich. A special thanks goes to Ron Weisen for his commentary, documents, and his spirit.

A major portion of the research for this book was carried out under a joint National Science Foundation/Centre National de Recherches Scientifiques Exchange of Scientists grant for 1981–1982. I wish to thank all those responsible for the grant and all those who assisted me in the research. They are too numerous to name individually, but they know who they are and how important they were to me.

L. E. R.

CONTENTS

PLANT CLOSINGS

Chapter 1

INTRODUCTION: MYTH, POWER, AND THE POLITICS OF PLANT CLOSINGS

Why is it that those with little political and economic power often accept—with an emotional and unquestioning attachment—political analyses, descriptions of economic and political conditions, and perceptions of themselves apparently detrimental to their own interest? Such detrimental analyses, descriptions, and perceptions are mythic because their necessity and factual support for them are ambiguous or illusory. Yet, by the acceptance of these perspectives, or myths, the power-poor ignore or diminish what power they do have and are even less able to defend themselves against the imposition of drastic and unequal reductions in their well-being.

The recent period of economic crisis and the responses by workers, governments, and business provide several interesting cases in which to test an explanation for these accepted perspectives and their consequences. Of particular interest is the relatively short life of the idea of an industrial policy in the United States, particularly an active policy for dealing with plant closings and economic layoffs.[1]

This situation raises several questions that we shall attempt to answer: Why has the drastic assault on their economic well-being that plant closings and economic layoffs represent not spurred workers to greater political and trade union militancy? Why have workers, their unions, and communities not been more active in pressing politically for plant closing and layoff regulation? When undertaken, why have such efforts been so half-hearted and unsuccessful? Why have such efforts not captured the imagination and support of most U.S. trade unionists? Why are the reactions of workers, their unions, and communities so different in the United States from those in other Western industrialized countries?

In attempting to answer these questions, let us first consider an explanatory hypothesis that stresses the importance of myth to power relations. Then in the second chapter we will review the economic conditions in the United States and France that would seem to require—and have already mandated in Europe—some form of layoff and plant closing regulation. Then, two cases of rejection of proposals for layoff and plant closing legislation, one in the United States and one in Rhode Island, will be presented in order to discover if myth played any role in the power relations that caused their rejection. These cases will be contrasted with the adoption of layoff regulation in France. Comparative analysis will explore the differing roles of myth in French and U.S. labor politics. Youngstown, Ohio, and Longwy, Lorraine, provide two cases of closings and numerous layoffs in the steel industry that highlight very different worker responses and suggest some explanation for these responses and their consequences. The second chapter will conclude with several recommendations that will be tested, revised, and/or confirmed in later chapters.

By means of comparative analysis, we shall describe the relationship between myth (that is, widely accepted analyses, conceptions, and perceptions with ambiguous or illusory factual support), worker militancy, the political power of workers, and industrial policy. The hypothesis suggests that certain myths (which will be explained later in more detail) sap worker militancy, thereby decreasing the political power of workers. Decreased worker power, in turn, reduces the saliency of the issue of industrial policy which, in effect, allows the establishment of an industrial policy by financiers and employers against the interests of workers. It is not the purpose of this book to prove conclusively this relationship; rather, we shall elicit evidence and suggest interpretations of that evidence which are often ignored when the U.S. experience is looked at in isolation and when the myths pervasive in that experience are accepted without question. At worst, the evidence and interpretations may show that very different myths with different political consequences may find equal support in the available economic evidence.

In order to see what role myth plays in political power, it is necessary to outline three aspects or faces of power and the different ways in which these aspects can be identified. These faces of power are not equally easy to identify. Often one or more of the faces is overlooked as a manifestation of power and is seen as an unassailable, natural condition of human life. If unassailable, then even those burdened by this condition are unlikely to challenge it and are apt to discourage the "quixotic" or "utopian" few who do.[2]

The First Face of Power: The Public Face

The first face of power, which we call the public and institutional face, is the most easily identifiable and the most visible. It is the power held by the public decision makers and the institutions legally charged with making important public decisions. This face of power operates on issues that are the focus of public attention and debate. We know of the participants, issues, and outcomes because we read about them in the newspaper, hear them on radio, and see them on television. Positions on the issues are taken by groups whose organizations and resources allow them to be heard and to influence the outcome of major decisions. The power of any individual or group is measured by the extent of its active and public participation in the decision and by the extent to which the outcome reflects its original position and interest. Those who are unheard are deemed to be either uninterested in the outcome or already represented in the decision-making process.[3]

Examples of the first face of power are obvious in major public debates on issues such as abortion, in the formal and legally binding decision making by legislators, judges, and executive branch officials, in the takeover of one large corporation by another, and, of course, in the invasion and occupation of one country by the armed forces of another. In industrial relations, the first face of power is easily identified in the contest of organized labor and management in collective bargaining, strikes, lockouts, lawsuits, and union elections. In labor politics, it is identified in the lobbying of organized labor and business for legislation, the endorsement and support of candidates for elective or appointive office, and the participation of labor and business leaders on civic and governmental bodies. The important issues and actors are readily identified and the modes of action are familiar and highly visible. We see them on the evening news.

The Second Face of Power: The Power to Suppress

Because the first face of power is so familiar and visible and because its visibility provides a major justification for existing institutions, it is often regarded as the essence and totality of all power relations. Like an iceberg, however, many aspects or types of power are not accessible to public scrutiny. Other faces of power exist that are not openly discussed on the evening news because they are exercised negatively, by keeping issues and interests from becoming subjects of formal and public decision making.

Thus, a second face of power appears when one looks at which people and issues are left out of public decision making.[4] Power in this respect means the barriers and roadblocks that preclude or make difficult the public participation of some groups and the appearance of some issues, thereby preventing challenges to the status quo and to the participating elites from certain quarters. The exercise of power is beyond public scrutiny in corporate boardrooms, private clubs, and millions of economic transactions. Such power, as possessed by the banking industry for example, can be exercised in a generalized and impersonal way. In selecting criteria for investment and in choosing particular investments, the industry can condemn entire cities, areas of endeavor, or groups of people to economic impotence and decay. Those condemned may not be the immediate subjects of negative decisions, but rather the indirect victims of the allocation of resources elsewhere. Although their struggle is less overt, they are no less disadvantaged by power relations than the worker in a one-company town who is evicted from company-owned housing after losing his or her job over a personal dispute with the boss.

Michael Parenti, John Gaventa, and others have documented that "[o]ne of the most important aspects of power [is] not to prevail in a struggle but to predetermine the agenda of struggle— to determine whether certain questions ever reach the competitive stage."[5] These studies, inquiring into the political inaction in the face of evident grievances of groups such as urban and rural blacks and unemployed Appalachian miners, demonstrated the effects of the dominance of local elites. The elites used various formal and informal controls to punish, hinder, or prevent political organization or involvement. Their influence over the local news media greatly reduced and distorted coverage of many issues of importance to workers, the poor, and the unemployed. Over time they were also able to erode gains that episodic political action had won for the subordinate groups.

Given these resources in the hands of the elites, inaction often resulted without the need for overt coercion because of the anticipated high costs and expected failure of political action on the part of the aggrieved groups. The power to set the local political agenda was often twice removed from the subordinate groups because that agenda was set first by absentee corporations and then embellished and implemented by local political and business leaders serving the absentee interests while trying also to further their own. Thus, air and water pollution in Gary, Indiana, and the undertaxation and rape of land held by the British-owned American Association in Appalachia were rarely, if ever, local political issues despite the fact that important segments of the population were being very adversely affected.

In Youngstown, after the closing of a major steel plant, many laid-off workers expressed their fear that political involvement in the buy-out movement might jeopardize their unemployment benefits, while workers still employed in plants where major layoffs had been announced feared that political action would cause them to be singled out for dismissal. In Longwy, this second face of power appeared in the refusal of the government and the steel companies to negotiate jointly with the unions and in their constant claim in separate negotiations that each important issue was only in the power of the other actor.[6]

Power was being exercised to prevent the appearance of certain issues and the organization and recognition of certain aggrieved groups. Similarly, industrial relations often does not recognize unemployed workers, unorganized workers, and even the rank and file of many unions as active participants in the organization. Both business and union leaders often exercise power in such a way as to limit the influence of these groups. Their interests are not generally represented in collective bargaining or in the lobbying of labor and business organizations. Furthermore, these groups are not independently organized or represented although their stake in industrial relations and in all business and labor legislation is often extremely large.

The power to suppress in the industrial setting is best described by a business leader himself. In a 1971 *Harvard Business Review* article, "Why Motivation Theory Won't Work," Thomas Fitzgerald, Director of Employee Research and Training for the Chevrolet Division of General Motors, cautions against job enrichment and worker participation efforts because they lead to challenges to management prerogatives and the power of capital. Fitzgerald notes that meaningful work reform must include the redesign of jobs and the production process with the participation of workers and with worker access to sensitive corporate information. But even small beginnings in this direction would seriously threaten management's power and, therefore, must be avoided. He states:[7]

> *Once competence is shown (or believed to be shown) in, say, rearranging the work area, and after participation has become a conscious, officially sponsored activity, participators may well want to go on to topics of job assignment, the allocation of rewards, or even the selection of leadership. In other words, management's present monopoly—on initiating participation, on the nomination of conferees, and on the limitations of legitimate areas of review—can itself easily become a source of contention.*

Fitzgerald argues that such issues should never be brought up and should be immediately discouraged if brought up by labor. The managerial power noted in Fitzgerald's article often causes an anticipated reaction among workers and unions that suppresses demands for greater control of the job and the workplace and focuses upon wage demands that do not threaten managerial prerogatives. Job security demands are similarly blocked and displaced because unemployment, or the threat thereof, is the ultimate sanction behind managerial power.

Three Myths Rooted in the Second Face of Power

This book will show how three myths have their roots partly in the second face of power; that is, in the power of business interests to set the political and economic agenda to which trade unions must react and to suppress certain issues and groups, sometimes with the assistance of trade union leaders. We will call these the "myth of big labor," the "myth of the business climate," which includes the subsidiary "myth of foreign competition," and the "myth of legality."

The myth of big labor emphasizes the excessive political and economic power of trade unions. The power of trade unions is deemed to be excessive because it is unnecessary for the protection of workers, adds unnecessary costs and inflexibility to business activities, decreases the ability of businesses to compete with nonunion and foreign enterprises, is able to create and adopt an antibusiness political agenda, has unwarranted influence over political candidates, and has been acquired and maintained by a corrupt and authoritarian leadership.[8]

In Chapter 2, we will demonstrate that the evidence to support this myth is either nonexistent or exaggerated. First we will examine the actual influence of the labor movement on the issue of plant closing and layoff protection and the extent to which the myth of big labor itself affected that influence by the suppression of important issues and interests. Additional evidence will be gleaned from a brief investigation of the origin of the idea of excessive trade union power and by showing what influence and success the labor movement has had generally in realizing its political and economic agenda. The interpretation of the evidence that important issues and interests were suppressed must be further considered in the light of the French comparison in Chapter 3.

The business climate myth is grounded in the idea that any move by government or trade unions to aid workers or to strengthen the labor movement is an illegitimate burden upon the profitability of business and reduces the attractiveness to investment of the jurisdiction (usually the state) in which the move is made. The myth is generally used as an argument or reason for opposing policies favorable to workers and for opposing trade union activity. It is said that if such a policy or activity is undertaken, business profitability will suffer, businesses will not invest, expand, or open in the state, and jobs will be lost. In the extreme, the myth is presented to suggest that plant closings and layoffs are caused by measures to prevent or limit plant closings and layoffs.[9]

The cases presented in Chapters 2, 3, and 4 will serve to illustrate many situations in which this myth is "trotted out" to oppose the political and economic agenda of both French and American workers. Using the evidence of these cases and additional evidence gleaned from survey data, interviews, and economic analysis, we will evaluate what truth lies in the myth and to what extent it is used to suppress or distort important facts and issues.

The myth of legality is grounded in the notion that the legal system is neutral, and hence fair, in its handling of issues which affect workers, that the justice of the law reflects the same values as the workers' sense of justice, and that the law "means what it says." There is, however, a range of ideological limitations on the legal rights of workers to participate in the important decisions of business policy that directly affect them. These limitations can be loosely gathered under the rubric of "management prerogatives" that stem from the notion that ownership and property extend to the control of capital. Even legislation such as the National Labor Relations Act of 1935 (NLRA), which in the plain meaning of its language seems to counter some of the prerogatives of capital, has always been limited by and judicially interpreted in light of the power of capital to set the terms upon which labor sells its activity.[10]

The Supreme Court has clearly stated that the NLRA does not establish an equal right of workers and employers to make decisions about the running of the business in which they are employed.[11] Despite this, the NLRA is deemed to establish "industrial democracy." The mythical character of the legal constructs that underlie American labor law is further highlighted when the American form of industrial democracy is compared to the forms of worker participation either established or advocated by workers abroad. These latter forms of participation have much more in common with popularly accepted notions of the meaning of the word "democracy."

We will examine cases for evidence of the extent to which the promises made to workers in the law serve to obscure and suppress important issues surrounding the actual power relations of workers and employers. This evidence can be found in the debates surrounding the adoption, rejection, or amendment of the law, in court and administrative cases, and in the use and enforcement of the law.

The Third Face of Power: Myth Internalized

The myth of big labor, the myth of the business climate, and the myth of legality are partly rooted in the second face of power because they fortify institutional and public biases against the raising of certain issues and the participation of certain groups. When these myths are accepted and internalized by those against whom they operate, they serve to block or cloud the perception of grievances and of viable options for resolving the grievances. This, then, is the third face of power.

Subordinate groups come to accept their powerlessness and the illegitimacy or inexpressibility of their grievances. They accept as natural and unchallengeable the practices and rationales that guarantee their subordination despite vague rumblings of dissatisfaction ("troubles") with the status quo. This dissatisfaction may even manifest itself in hatred and action against others who more visibly challenge the status quo and who are more vulnerable to the actions of nonelites. It is here at the intersection of power and consciousness that myth plays a key role.[12]

It is evident that to the extent that workers accept the myths of big labor and business climate, they will be less likely to perceive any value in plant closing and layoff regulation, greater worker control, and increased union activity and militancy. Workers will be equally reluctant to support efforts of the labor movement to link its struggle to the struggles of other groups, such as environmentalists, minorities, antiwar activists and women, who are seeking to restrict the power of business to invest and manage its affairs without concern for their interests. By accepting these myths, workers will have deprived themselves of alternative analyses that might win support for their interests from important institutions and the public. Workers who accept the myths of big labor and of the business climate will perceive solidarity as a danger rather than a value. The acceptance of the myths counsels inaction and concession to the demands of business.

The myth of legality, if accepted, functions in a similar way. Grievances are perceived as isolated disputes fully resolvable by a fair and impartial body. Little attention is paid to the power relations from which the disputes arise and the continuing nature of those power relations beyond settlement of a particular dispute. Trade union militance to affect these power relations is sapped as workers either sit back expecting a court or administrative tribunal to settle the matter or remain tied up in the procedural complexities of the legal system. If the legal system is not fair and impartial, if its impartiality is based on its implicit acceptance of the existing power relations, or if its accessibility is overestimated, the result is inaction, frustrations, and loss of the sense that the workers' grievances are legitimate.

In the cases and examples presented in this book, evidence of the third face of power and its effects will be sought in the statements of workers, labor leaders, and the unemployed. These statements come from interviews, participant observation, court and legislative hearing transcripts, meeting minutes, and the press. This evidence will be supplemented by recently available survey data comparing attitudes of French and American workers.[13]

Interpretations, Conclusions, and Recommendations

In the final chapter, the evidence elicited in the preceding chapters will be analyzed and interpreted to see what light, if any, can be shed on why American workers and their unions have not been more militant in pursuing their goals and why those goals have not generally included strong and effective demands for greater job security and for greater control over investment decisions. The chapter will draw conclusions about the extent to which the faces of power, and particularly the more obscure second and third faces, operate through the myths of big labor, business climate, and legality to suppress workers' demands and to sap their militancy. The comparison of the French and American experiences will help us gauge the effects of greater or lesser militancy on the furthering of workers' interests.

Finally, the chapter will look at the belief structure that underlies the myths presented, seeking their origin in more fundamental aspects of economics, politics, and culture. In doing so, intimations of the future of the American and French labor movements will be more fully developed, along with recommendations for improving that future.

Endnotes

1. See e.g., Gerald Glyde, "Managing Economic Change: Labor's Role," in Donald Kennedy (ed.), *Labor and Reindustrialization: Workers and Corporate Change* (University Park: Pennsylvania State Univ., Dept. of Labor Studies, 1984), pp. 1–25.
2. See e.g., William Connolly, "Appearance and Reality," *Political Theory* 7 (Nov. 1969), pp. 445–68.
3. For the development of power studies focusing on this aspect of power only, see Nelson Polsby, *Community Power and Political Theory* (New Haven,

Conn.: Yale Univ. Press, 1963) and Robert Dahl, *Pluralist Democracy in the United States: Conflict and Consent* (Chicago: Rand McNally, 1967).

4. Peter Bachrach and Morton Baratz, *Power and Poverty: Theory and Practice* (New York: Oxford Univ. Press, 1970); Steven Lukes, *Power: A Radical View* (London: MacMillan, 1974); E. E. Schattschneider, *The Semi-Sovereign People: A Realist's View of Democracy* (New York: Holt, Rinehart & Winston, 1960).

5. Michael Parenti, "Power and Pluralism: A View from the Bottom," *Journal of Politics*, 32 (1970), pp. 501–30; John Gaventa, *Power and Powerlessness: Quiescence and Rebellion in an Appalachian Valley* (Urbana: Univ. of Illinois Press, 1980); Matthew Crenson, *The Un-Politics of Air Pollution: A Study of Non-Decision Making in the Cities* (Baltimore: Johns Hopkins Univ. Press, 1971).

6. See Chapter 4.

7. Thomas Fitzgerald, "Why Motivation Theory Won't Work," *Harvard Business Review* (July–August 1971), pp. 37–43 at 43; cf. Schattschneider, note 4, ch. 4 on "The Displacement of Conflicts" and Michael Best and William Connolly, *The Politicized Economy* (Lexington, Mass.: D.C. Heath, 1982), pp. 140–44.

8. James Atleson, *Values and Assumptions in American Labor Law* (Amherst: Univ. of Massachusetts Press, 1983), pp. 146–48.

9. The most active purveyor of this myth in Rhode Island is Joseph Goodrich, business editor and columnist for the *Providence Journal*. See quotes in Chapter 2.

10. See e.g., *NLRB v. Mackay Radio & Telegraph Co.*, 304 U.S. 333 (1938); Karl Klare, "Judicial Deradicalization of the Wagner Act and the Origins of Modern Legal Consciousness, 1937–41," *Minnesota Law Review*, 62 (1978), pp. 265–339; Atleson, note 8, pp. 1–16; cf. Bernard Edelman, *La Légalisation de la Class Ouvrière* (Paris: Christian Bourgois Editeur, 1978), pp. 23–30, discussing the similar development of French labor law.

11. *First National Maintenance Corp. v. NLRB*, 452 U.S. 666,676 (1981).

12. Connolly, note 7, pp. 446–48; cf. Lukes, note 4.

13. I am especially indebted to Olivier Kourchid for his aid and for *Les Ouvrièrs entre la Crise et l'Enteprise* (Paris: Groupe de Sociologie du Travail, 1984) which reports this attitudinal survey data.

Chapter 2

MYTH, POWER, AND PLANT CLOSING LEGISLATION IN THE UNITED STATES

In this chapter we will examine several attempts to pass plant closing and layoff legislation in order to determine the power relations that caused the issues to be raised and to be resolved in the way they were. Key facts that emerge from the cases are the outcome (i.e., failure to pass the legislation) and the lack of enthusiasm and militancy of organized labor in working for its passage.

Looking solely at the first, public face of power would simply lead to the conclusion that business interests mustered more public and official support for their view and were more effective in defending their interests on this issue than organized labor was. This approach, however, only scratches the surface of the explanation. Why was the business position able to attract so much public and official support and, most importantly, why did this position attract the support of so many workers and trade unionists? In trying to answer these questions, we will occasionally glimpse the second and third faces of power and the myths of big labor, of the business climate and of legality operating behind the scenes.

Labor's Interest in the Regulation of Plant Closings and Layoffs

First, it is necessary to establish the existence of economic conditions that would reasonably generate a strong interest of workers

13

and trade unions in plant closing and layoff regulation. If such conditions exist, then the failure to recognize and to act vigorously on that interest must be explained. We will look at the cases for an explanation.

While the available data do not allow the precise determination of the effect of plant closings on industrial employment, the data do suggest what interests of workers, trade unions, and local governments are jeopardized by economic dislocation. From 1969 to 1976 the United States suffered a net loss of 1.2 million manufacturing jobs. After a brief recovery between 1976 and 1980, the number of manufacturing jobs again plunged by 2.3 million between 1980 and 1985. It is estimated that 90% of these lost jobs will never be recovered.[1]

Barry Bluestone and Bennett Harrison in their book *The Deindustrialization of America,* using data obtained by David Birch from the accounts of Dun & Bradstreet, estimate that between 1967 and 1976 1.6 million business closings engendered the loss of 22 million jobs. They add to this figure another 16 million jobs lost from reductions in force not directly attributable to closings. The number of workers laid off, the percentage of laid-off workers among the unemployed, and the average duration of unemployment have all greatly increased since 1969. More than half of the 1979 workforce of the automobile and steel industries has been laid off. While the national unemployment rate has dropped from a 1983 high of well over 10%, the recovery is uneven and fragile, and the number of discouraged workers approaches 2 million.[2]

Although the number of lost jobs has generally been counterbalanced by the number of new jobs created (except from 1974 to 1975 and 1980 to 1983), the new jobs are more likely to be less well paid, less skilled, less unionized, only part-time, and located in regions of the country other than those suffering most from job destruction and unemployment. The United States has undergone a more profound shift of employment toward the tertiary sector (primarily toward services and retail sales) than other industrialized countries. From 1973 to 1982, more than 70% of new employment occurred in these branches of activity.

Moreover, from 1960 to 1982, 66% of new employment was generated by enterprises of fewer than 20 employees. During the 1970s, 62% of laid-off blue-collar workers were highly skilled. These figures indicate that the branches in which the greatest increase in employment occurred were those in which salaries were generally lower and where the salaries in real dollars had stagnated or declined. Furthermore the branches in which employment rose were characterized by an extremely low level of skill requirements and of unionization and a high proportion of part-time positions.[3]

Finally, the loss of industrial jobs has important regional effects because the creation of new industrial employment has advanced more slowly in the older industrial states of the Northeast and the Midwest than in the other regions of the country. Between 1969 and 1976, the Northeast and Midwest lost 1.5 million industrial jobs while the other regions saw the creation of 300,000 such jobs.[4]

The "recovery" of 1984 has not reduced economic dislocation. Business failures have increased. The number of discouraged workers and the number of those who have exhausted their unemployment insurance without finding employment are at all-time highs since the depression. While job replacement has increased nationally, the hardest hit states of the Northeast and Midwest still have unemployment rates considerably higher than the national average and some as high or higher than in 1983. The replacement jobs are again nonindustrial, less skilled, lower paying, and very often part-time. All these statistics fail to account for the devastating effects of unemployment and plant closings on workers, their families, and their communities. The effects on mental and physical health, marital and family relations, and community vitality are only now beginning to be well documented by systematic and journalistic studies.[5]

The new jobs created by the restructuring of employment have not matched the destroyed jobs either in number or quality. Furthermore, there is a lag in the reemployment of resources after disinvestment. Many case studies have shown that unemployment as a result of a plant closing, especially during an economic recession, is of long duration and has permanent effects on the earnings of workers.[6] The loss of tax revenues and the costs of providing benefits and services to the unemployed in communities hard-hit by plant closings far exceed the new revenues available to communities where employment is expanded. The medical, psychological, and social problems created in a community hit by massive and sudden unemployment are evident, but not easily quantified. Not so evident are the social costs of new and unplanned boom towns unorganized to cope with new demands on services and scarce resources.

Existing Worker Protection

The strong interest in plant closing and layoff regulation that these
economic conditions would be expected to arouse might be
ameliorated by job protections and benefits for laid-off workers
achieved through existing legislation and collective bargaining
agreements. In some instances, existing benefits have operated
to quell or delay strong worker opposition to layoffs and closings.
In general, however, there are no legal limitations on plant closings or mass economic layoffs beyond those which may have
been negotiated in collective bargaining agreements. The
Supreme Court has held that an employer is not required to
bargain over a partial or total plant shutdown resulting from
economic circumstances unless specific contractual language
requires it.[7]

Fewer than 14% of the collective bargaining agreements in
manufacturing industries have any such contractual language
limiting the right of an employer to close a plant or reduce
operations substantially. Most of the contracts that touch on the
subject require only that the employer negotiate on the conditions
of employees' termination and not on alternatives to it. Regarding
notice of layoffs, approximately 15% of all collective bargaining
agreements require more than one week of notice in advance of
dismissal. Fewer than 40% of collective bargaining agreements
require severance pay when an employee is dismissed for reasons
other than his own fault. Where severance pay is part of a contract, it is generally equal to between two and eight weeks of
salary depending on the years of service.[8]

The legal standing of even these minimal protections is doubt-
ful. In 1984, the Supreme Court ruled that a collective bargaining
agreement does not necessarily survive the closing or sale of an
enterprise unless the survival of the agreement and the conditions
of that survival are specifically addressed in the contract. Furthermore, the agreements do not necessarily survive the reorganization of the enterprise under the bankruptcy laws. The courts and
the National Labor Relations Board (NLRB) have also rejected the
notion that collective bargaining agreements prevent the transfer
of work to other facilities, even if the transfer leads to mass layoffs
in the original facility.[9] In any case, collective bargaining agreements, whether or not addressing plant closings and economic

layoffs, cover only about 25% of all workers and 49% of those in manufacturing.[10]

Some unions have succeeded in limiting or conditioning the power of an employer to close a plant. Contracts between the International Brotherhood of Electrical Workers (IBEW) and Westinghouse presently require two years of notice prior to a total or partial plant closing. The IBEW–Westinghouse agreements also give the union limited access to information on the company's investment projects. Contracts between the United Food and Commercial Workers and several meat packers prohibit the re-opening of a plant within five years of its initial closing without unionization. The Amalgamated Clothing and Textile Workers Union and the Clothing Manufacturing Association have nego-tiated a contractual provision prohibiting the employer from relocating an establishment during the period of the contract.

Sixteen percent of collective bargaining agreements, notably those of the United Auto Workers (UAW) and the United Steel Workers of America (USWA), contain provisions that guarantee, with the aid of some governmental programs discussed below, the payment of 70–90% of the salary of a laid-off worker for one year following his dismissal.[11] In the most recent round of con-tract negotiations, employers have demanded that these benefits be reduced. In their 1982 concession bargaining with the auto-makers, the UAW attempted to negotiate job security provisions but failed to achieve any substantial job guarantees in the face of threatened layoffs. Although they placed job security items at the top of their agenda in their 1984 contract efforts, auto workers achieved little success in getting them written into the contract.

While some collective bargaining agreements have provided protection to workers facing a plant closing, most agreements have eliminated the right to strike over the possibility or the conditions of a shutdown. Since the 1950s, most collective bar-gaining agreements have included a provision requiring that all disputes arising under the contract be submitted to arbitration. In exchange for agreeing to arbitration, employers have generally insisted on and received a provision prohibiting strikes during the term of the contract. In the face of recent closings, the courts have interpreted the "no strike clause" to mean that the union had renounced its right to strike on all issues while the contract was in force. On the other hand, the closing of a plant has been considered a management prerogative linked to common law property rights, not arising under the contract and not subject to the arbitration clause. This asymmetric relationship leaves workers powerless to act outside the limits of their contracts and, at the same time, unprotected by the contracts in the face of a plant closing.[12]

To note the dearth of statutory and contractual limitations on plant closings is not to say that a worker laid off in a shutdown is totally without resources. Since the depression there have been aid programs to assist the unemployed and destitute. The Unemployment Insurance (UI) program provides an initial 26 weeks of benefits and the possibility of receiving extended benefits for another 23 weeks.

While the professed goal of the UI program has been to replace 50% of the recipient's lost salary until he or she finds a suitable job (i.e., a job that allows the worker to maintain or improve his or her job skills and standard of living), this goal has rarely been achieved. The maximum weekly UI benefits range from a little over $200 in some states to under $100 in others. In 1982, when unemployment was at record, postdepression levels and more than 40% of those receiving benefits exhausted them before finding another job, the Reagan administration raised the levels of unemployment that must be recorded in a state before extended benefits may be paid.[13]

The Trade Adjustment Assistance Program of the Trade Readjustment Act of 1962 (TRA) was intended for the special case of those unemployed as a result of foreign competition. If a worker could demonstrate that the competition of foreign products in the U.S. market "significantly contributed" to her or his unemployment, the worker was eligible to receive: (1) 65% of his or her average weekly salary for 52 weeks, (2) job retraining, and (3) an allowance for relocation to where job prospects are better.

The TRA was only marginally effective. From 1962 to 1974, only 30,000 workers were declared eligible for the program because of an extremely narrow interpretation of the phrase "significantly contributed." The phrase was interpreted to mean that foreign competition was the necessary and sufficient cause of the worker's unemployment. The Trade Act of 1974 liberalized this interpretation, raised the maximum benefits, and added an allocation for the expenses of seeking new employment. Between 1980 and 1982, over 500,000 workers were eligible for the program. Since 1982, the funding for the program has been cut 70% by reestablishing the earlier interpretation, by reducing TRA benefits to the level of UI benefits, and by paying the benefits only after those of UI have been exhausted.[14]

After exhausting UI or TRA benefits, an unemployed person is sometimes eligible for welfare. Aid for Families with Dependent Children–Unemployed (AFDC–U) and General Assistance furnish benefits to families and single persons who earn an average of less than $5000 annually and who have no other assets of value such as a house, car, savings account, or insurance policy. This last condition is particularly onerous for the unemployed because it requires them to forfeit assets they accumulated during their prior working days in order to assure a less than modest income for their families. In many cases, this situation is forced on the unemployed because they have lost their job-related health coverage and must be eligible for public assistance in order to also be eligible for Medicaid. For example, at the peak of the recession (January 1983), 32 million people had lost their health coverage as a result of unemployment.[15]

It is evident that the protections for the workers against severe deprivation and hardship are minimal at best. Even those who avail themselves of these programs temporarily and eventually find work suffer large reductions in their earning capacity and their financial reserves.[16] Existing legislation is inadequate, and collective bargaining has not generally been effective in preventing or even greatly lessening these hardships.

Even before the Reagan administration's cutbacks in the programs available to aid workers hit by plant closings and layoffs, the programs were never adequate to deal with an economic crisis of any magnitude. The programs were designed as temporary, stopgap measures for industry-specific slack periods and short-term unemployment. In addition, the measures do not constitute a comprehensive industrial policy. Existing programs are inadequate to cope with a widespread recession and long-term unemployment that will constitute a massive but unplanned restructuring of American industry and job distribution.

What the foregoing description of existing conditions suggests is that workers have been badly hurt by plant closings and large-scale economic layoffs. Furthermore, existing statutory and contractual powers and protections are not adequate to prevent, reduce, or ameliorate the effects of the layoffs and plant closings. Objectively, then, the passage of legislation regulating plant closings and layoffs would seem to serve important interests of workers and the labor movement.

Union Leaders' Views: The Joint Labor Union
Study Tour of Europe

Leaders of major trade unions recognized that plant closing and
layoff legislation, as well as more economic planning and regulation of corporate activities, would be in the interest of workers
and the labor movement. Interestingly, this awareness was made
most explicit in the comparison between U.S. industrial policy
and that of Sweden, West Germany, and the United Kingdom.
Representatives of the United Auto Workers, the United Steel
Workers, and the International Association of Machinists (IAM)
participated in a tour of the three European countries, studying
their handling of plant closings and economic dislocation. As a
result of the Labor Union Study Tour, in 1979 the three unions
jointly published a list of 27 recommendations for dealing with
economic dislocation in the United States.[17]

The three union presidents, Douglas Fraser of the UAW, Lloyd
McBride of the USWA, and William Winpisinger of the IAM,
endorsed the recommendations of the report. The endorsements
of Fraser and Winpisinger are strong statements of the interest
workers and the labor movement have in plant closing and layoff
regulation. The statement of Lloyd McBride, however, indicates
a withdrawal from the recommendations. The implications of
McBride's coolness will be discussed later. Fraser declares:[18]

> *Few decisions in our complex interdependent society have farther
> reaching or more profound impact than decisions to close or move a
> plant. Yet these decisions are made behind closed boardroom doors,
> beyond public scrutiny or control, based solely on corporate eco-
> nomic self-interest, and without adequate regard to the enormous
> economic and social costs which such decisions can impose on others.
> We believe government has a duty to inject social responsibility into
> these decisions, to protect workers and communities against their
> devastating impact. New and comprehensive federal legislation to
> achieve this goal is badly needed.*

This is not only a recognition of the interest of workers in such
legislation, but the first paragraph is also an explicit recognition of
the second face of power (the power to suppress) in operation. It
is important to note that a major theme of the recommendations
of the study tour was the disclosure of corporate information
making formerly hidden issues and decisions public.

Characteristically, William Winpisinger's statement is even stronger. It not only recognizes workers' interest in plant closing and

layoff regulation but also reflects Winpisinger's recognition and condemnation of the myths of big labor, the business climate, and legality because of their devastating political and economic consequences. As we will see later, Winpisinger's analysis has much in common with that of French trade unionists. For this reason, his statement will be quoted at length:[19]

Economic Dislocation is too nice a term to describe the human anxiety, misery and tragedy that occur when corporate employers pack up and leave town in pursuit of maximum profits. It's professional economists' jargon for going soft on the Corporate State.

In the United States, we can call it what it is—subversion of the economy with intent to overthrow industrial democracy.

What else can we say, when we see our industrial communities blighted with abandoned plants and factories? When we see the industrial landscape cratered with depressed areas? When we see our union members stranded in the desolate halls of unemployment offices or Trade Adjustment Assistance lines? When we see our corporate employers speeding from our communities and our shores, in irrational flight from trade unions and collective bargaining; from wage and hour standards; from occupational safety and health standards; from environmental protection standards? When we see our corporate employers directly investing capital at a $25 billion annual rate overseas, then blaming U.S. workers for low productivity? When we see our corporate employers colluding with autocratic and dictatorial governments in developing and underdeveloped countries to produce and manufacture for export back to the U.S. market, in violation of human rights and even minimal standards of economic and social justice? When we see our employers practicing corporate cannibalism by raiding and acquiring other firms and enterprises, and committing corporate incest by merging with each other, only to leave workers and communities orphaned and stranded as they spin-off, shutdown and move established plants and facilities, in quest of profit maximization?

Sweden, West Germany and Great Britain, basically, feature capitalistic and market economies. Yet, the inherent lust for profit and power is checked by a humane concern for labor, collective bargaining and free trade unionism. Economic planning, and worker participation in that planning, are central to their systems. So is government regulation.

The recommendations found at the end of this report are instructive and necessary, if the United States is to remain a viable industrial democracy. They are commended to those who have a sincere interest in improving the American Economic System and to those who recognize the need for corporate employers to be held socially accountable to workers and their communities.

The recommendations call for several measures that have been incorporated into plant closing bills at the state and federal levels. (A complete list of the recommendations of the Labor Union Study Tour can be found in the Appendix of this chapter.) These measures include notice at least one year in advance of a plant closing or major reduction in operations; stiff penalties for failure to give notice, to provide required information, or to make mandated payments; programs for short-time work and overtime and hiring freezes; and improved monetary, transfer, placement, and training assistance for the readjustment of workers whose jobs are in jeopardy. The recommendations call for a higher level "safety net" for those threatened with or suffering from layoffs and for communities hard-hit by unemployment.

The recommendations urge substantially improved availability of economic information, both in the form of corporate financial planning data and governmental studies of development possibilities, economic dislocation, and labor market structure. Greater access to corporate information is a necessary preliminary to greater public and worker participation in business decision making. It makes public uses of power that were previously hidden within the enterprise and behind unassessable claims of economic necessity.

Several recommendations provide for the possibility of federal intervention in three areas: (1) control of a portion of the investment of large corporations, (2) supervision of mergers and acquisitions to achieve employment goals, and (3) supervision of foreign investment in order to protect both American workers from job export and foreign workers from exploitation. Recommendation 27 mentions, without elaboration, the creation of "appropriate labor market bodies" and "workplace adjustment and planning groups [to] coordinate implementation of the . . . recommendations." Under certain conditions these entities could be the instruments of a planned, comprehensive industrial policy, at the macro- and micro-levels, in which workers and all levels of government have a significant voice.

The recommendations are vague as to the mechanisms and institutions necessary for achieving the policy goals. They are not radical in that they do not call for nationalization, worker self-management, comprehensive and directed national planning, or an incomes policy similar to that of Western Europe. They do, however, provide for a much more public, planned, and worker-oriented approach to economic policy and business regulation than is presently the case in the United States. Fraser, Winpisinger, and the trade unionists on the study tour clearly see that such an approach is in the interest of workers and their trade unions.

A Legislative Model: The National Employment Priorities Act

How does proposed plant closing and layoff legislation address the economic interests of workers and trade unions? The legislation appears to tentatively reflect some of the concerns recognized by the study tour participants and the union leaders.

The most comprehensive proposals for federal or state legislation address some of the study tour recommendations but step back from those that embrace the more interventionist European legislative and regulatory schemes. There are no labor market planning bodies, investment controls, employment-oriented merger limitations, or mandatory job-listing provisions. The advance notice and reporting requirements of the proposed legislation (e.g., the National Employment Priorities Act of 1979) are a first step in requiring that business, government, and labor engage in a more open, planned, and participatory restructuring of an enterprise, an industry, and eventually the national economy. The income maintenance, redevelopment fund, retraining, early retirement, and transfer provisions would only begin dealing with the prevention of long-term unemployment created by industrial restructuring. Finally, the investigative, technical assistance, and buy-out provisions would help to limit job destruction.

The many different plant closing bills that have been presented at the state and federal levels are to a great extent patterned on (and whittled down from) the federal bill considered to be a model by the supporters of legislative action against plant closings. The National Employment Priorities Act of 1979 (NEPA) was proposed in the Senate by Donald Riegle (D–Mich.) and in the House by William Ford (D–Mich.).[20] The bill is an updated and reworked version of one presented by Representative Ford and then Senator Walter Mondale (D–Minn.) in 1974 that was never voted out of committee.[21]

The NEPA encompasses all establishments employing 50 or more persons and contemplating a closing or modification of activities that would result in the reduction of employment for at least 15% of the employees. The reduction need not be a layoff but might include a reduction in hours worked. The employer must give written notice of the modifications to the Secretary of Labor, the workers and unions at the establishment, and the affected local governments. The timing of the notice depends on the number of workers affected by the modification. If more than 500 are affected, the notice must be given at least two years prior to the closing or reduction of employment. If 100 to 500 are affected, the notice must be given 18 months in advance. If fewer than 100 workers are affected, six months' advance notice is required.

The notice provisions require more than a simple warning of the pending closing or reduction in employment. They must include a report on the reasons and expected effects of the modification of activities. The notice must specify: (1) the nature of the establishment where the reduction in employment will take place, (2) the reasons for the reduction, (3) possible alternatives to the reduction, (4) any requests made for governmental assistance, (5) the estimated magnitude of the reduction in employment, (6) measures taken to minimize the effects of the reduction of employment on the employees and on the affected local economy, (7) the economic condition of the establishment including its profitability and projected investment plans, (8) the economic circumstances of the larger enterprise, if any, to which the establishment belongs and the possibility of transferring employees to other establishments of the enterprise, and (9) the names and addresses of all employees affected by the reduction in employment.

The bill provides that if 10% of the employees or a union at the establishment request it, or if the Secretary of Labor deems it prudent, the secretary must conduct an inquiry on the points addressed in the notice and must publish the results of the inquiry along with recommendations. The secretary is authorized to inspect all the records of the establishment and of the enterprise with which it is affiliated. This provision represents a significant change from the 1974 bill, which gave the secretary authority to make findings as to the justifiability of a closing or reduction of operations and to impose sanctions on actions he or she deemed unjustified. The lack of standards for determining the justifiability of a shutdown or reduction of activities was used as one of the major arguments against the 1974 bill.

The 1979 version of the NEPA requires the employer to assure affected employees 85% of their previous salary for at least one year following their dismissal or reduction in hours worked. The employer must also continue making contributions for medical insurance and pensions during the year following the layoff. The bill gives affected employees rights to transfer to other establishments controlled by the enterprise if comparable employment exists. Workers who accept a transfer receive their moving expenses from the employer. This constitutes another major difference from the 1974 bill, which envisioned these payments being provided by the federal government instead of by the employer.

Under the National Employment Priorities Act of 1979, an enterprise that closes or moves to another location must pay 85% of one year's taxes to each local government that would lose the revenues because of the closing. Furthermore, if an enterprise relocates to a foreign country, it must pay the U.S. government 300% of one year's lost federal tax revenues.

The NEPA establishes the role of federal intervention and assistance. It authorizes the federal government to provide job training for laid-off employees, expenses of a job search, access to specialized employment agencies, and counselling. Pursuant to the bill, the government may provide technical assistance, loans and directed federal procurement under advantageous conditions to businesses in difficulty and contemplating closing or a substantial reduction in operations. It also authorizes the federal government to furnish affected local governments with grants and loans for social services and public works designed to provide aid and jobs for the unemployed. To exercise these and other powers under the bill, a National Employment Priorities Administration was established under the Secretary of Labor. This administration is also charged with undertaking research on business investment policy and unemployment and with providing technical assistance to business and local governments.

The National Employment Priorities Act represents the collected wisdom of the supporters of plant closing legislation. The bills proposed at the state level generally borrow significantly from the 1979 or 1974 versions.

An Overview of Recent Plant Closing Legislation

The recent political history of plant closing legislation is primarily the history of bills that have not been passed and of the efforts to pass or block them. The efforts to pass the legislation gather their force from the macroeconomic context outlined at the outset of this chapter, as well as from direct, local experience with closings, massive layoffs, and the inadequacy of aid for the unemployed. In recounting this history, we can look for instances in which the myths of big labor, of the business climate, and of legality acted to block or defeat plant closing legislation and/or dampen the support of workers and unions for such legislation.

Do business representatives at legislative hearings, legislators, or trade unionists themselves suggest that organized labor already has excessive power that hampers business growth and the preservation of jobs? Do they argue that the increased business regulation that plant closing laws represent will make investment in a particular jurisdiction (state or nation) unattractive, thereby driving business growth and new jobs to other, less interventionist or less labor-oriented jurisdictions? Do they argue that existing laws and opportunities for collective bargaining are adequate to handle any legitimate claims that workers may have? If such arguments are found in this historical survey—and especially if they come from workers and trade unionists themselves—there is strong evidence that myth exists and that the less public faces of power are at work.

This recent history begins with an early, but short-lived, taste of victory—the adoption of the Trade Adjustment Assistance Program. This 1962 legislation was partly a response to the economic crisis in the textile industry. The textile crisis was industry-specific, however, and other sectors responded to the general Keynesian stimulation undertaken by the Kennedy administration. The pressures for a more sweeping response to the problem of plant closings diminished with the recovery of other industries.

Early Action in Maine

Maine, which had been hard hit by the textile crisis, experienced a similar crisis in the shoe industry during the recession of 1969–1970. By 1971, several shoe and leather goods factories had closed or severely curtailed operations. A coalition of unions, local government officials, and civic organizations pushed for the adoption of a law to lessen the disastrous effects of plant closings on workers and local communities. With only a feeble resistance from the business community (not yet mobilized to the extent it would soon be), the coalition was able to obtain passage of a law requiring worker notice and severance pay.

The law covers establishments with 100 or more employees that close or relocate their operations. It requires one month notice to all employees being laid off (a provision that was subsequently amended). As a penalty for failure to give the requisite notice, each laid-off employee who had worked at the company for at least three years was to receive one week's salary for each year of employment. It is important to note that the passage of this modest piece of plant closing legislation has had no noticeable effect on the attraction of new investment into the state.[22]

The unions involved in the efforts to pass the Maine law viewed its passage as a first step destined to be expanded in the future—in terms of both greater protection for workers and the success of similar legislation in other states and eventually at the national level. This view turned out to be incorrect for several reasons. The law itself did not aid those already unemployed. The support of those recently laid off, which was very strong at the beginning of the campaign, dwindled as they left the state, found other jobs, or became embittered over their worsening situation. After the recession of 1969–1970, the economy was improving and earlier fears of continuing recession and unemployment were forgotten in the hope of a rapid and substantial recovery. As a result, the unions relaxed their pressure.

The awakening of the resistance of the business community to plant closing legislation caused local Maine officials to fear the development of a bad business climate that would hurt their state's competitive position for attracting new business investment. The unions involved in the original campaign, most notably the Amalgamated Clothing and Textile Workers Union (ACTWU) (who had lost half of their members and who had seen the relocation of establishments to less unionized localities during the crisis in the textile and leather industries), accepted halfheartedly the arguments of the business community about the "New War Between the States" and about the business climate. In 1973, under pressure from the business community, the law was amended dropping the worker-notification requirement but making severance pay mandatory. (A 1981 amendment has restored the worker-notification requirement in cases where a firm relocates outside of the state.) The ACTWU soon began to direct its efforts toward national legislation.[23]

Initial Efforts at the National Level

At the start of the 1970s, the AFL-CIO had higher national priorities than plant closing legislation. It was lobbying for general labor law reform that would include the repeal of Secion 14(b) of the Taft–Hartley Act of 1947 outlawing closed shops and permitting states to prohibit union shops. For workers in industries such as steel, automobiles, textiles, and rubber, their unions and the AFL-CIO were lobbying for the liberalization of the Trade Adjustment Assistance Program. The labor federation was also advocating legislation on workers' health and safety and on securing retirement benefits. In the latter three efforts, the lobbying was generally successful; moreover, the leaders of the AFL-CIO were generally in agreement with business leaders that the proper governmental response to unemployment was to encourage private investment in industry.

To deal with plant closings, the AFL-CIO (as well as the generally more progressive UAW) advocated collective bargaining agreements that included measures such as supplemental unemployment benefits and advance notice of layoffs.[24] The USWA leadership, first under I. W. Abel and later under Lloyd McBride, responded to the third face of power (myth internalized). They accepted management's position, despite strong evidence to the contrary, that foreign imports were the major reason for job loss and that to discourage end-of-contract stockpiling of foreign steel, the USWA must give up its right to strike, not only during the contract period but after as well. This position, along with the creation of joint union–management productivity committees, was embodied in the Experimental Negotiating Agreement of 1973. The agreement was pushed through a meeting of local union presidents without debate and with no opportunity for the rank and file to vote on it. These moves failed to reduce steel imports.[25]

The recession of 1974 raised the problem of plant closings to a higher level of priority on the legislative agenda of organized labor. With the support of the textile, automobile, steel, and machinists unions, Senator Mondale and Representative Ford introduced the National Employment Priorities Act of 1974 into their respective chambers. This bill envisioned a two-year advance notice requirement; a National Employee Relocation Administration to conduct studies of closings; sanctions, in the form of recouping tax incentives, against unjustified closings; and benefits to laid-off workers and affected communities to be paid by the federal government.

The strong resistance of the business community was directed particularly at the advance notice requirements which it viewed as an infringement on management prerogatives. Other factors (such as the lukewarm support of the AFL-CIO, the distractions of Watergate, and a new Ford administration hostile to economic regulation) also led to the failure of the bill to get out of committee.

In addition to the effect of the myths of big labor and of the business climate, the bill faced two telling criticisms. The first was its failure to define and provide criteria for determining the justifiability of a closing. The second was the possibility that the bill would allow the government to be blackmailed into bailing out failing businesses regardless of the economic or job preservation prognosis for such an action.[26]

Increased Momentum in the States

After the failure of the National Employment Priorities Act and in anticipation of growing resistance from the business community at the national level, the supporters of legislation again turned their efforts toward the states. An initial success at the state level once more raised hopes of further successes. In 1975, Wisconsin passed a law requiring notice 60 days prior to the cessation, relocation, or reduction of the operations of an enterprise of 100 or more employees. The courts were authorized to impose a fine of $50 for each affected worker if the required notice was not given.

The passage of the Wisconsin law did not have immediate repercussions in other states largely because the Wisconsin campaign was a special case. It had profited from the traditional hostility toward large corporations of former miners and dairy farmers who supported the efforts of the steel, paper, wood, and textile workers' unions to get the bill passed. In spite of the successful and vigorous campaign, to date the law has not been enforced in Wisconsin. In 1983, the mandatory notice provisions were repealed and replaced with voluntary guidelines and incentives to business that provide new employment.[27]

The policy of the states regarding closings and rising unemployment has centered principally on incentives to enterprises

that would agree to remain, expand, or relocate within the state.[28]
Nevertheless, 1975 did see some reinforcement of the demands
for the regulation of plant closings. Several union locals and
community organizations in Ohio formed a coalition called the
Ohio Public Interest Campaign (OPIC). OPIC set itself the task
of organizing at the grass-roots resistance to closings and to tax
incentives for business.

After two years, during which the coalition took its campaign
door-to-door, to the media, to union meetings, and to the corridors of Ohio's general assembly, the first comprehensive state bill
on plant closings was introduced into the legislature by Senator
Michael Schwarzwalder (D–Columbus). The bill, called the
Community Readjustment Act, required that an employer of 100
or more workers give notice two years prior to a closing or a
reduction in operations, file a report on the effects and reasons for
the closing, provide one week's severance pay for every year of a
worker's employment with the company, and contribute an
amount equal to 10% of its annual payroll to a fund for the redevelopment of affected local economies.

In the legislative hearings, the strongest supporting testimony
was given by the president of the International Union of Electrical Workers, David Fitzmaurice. The members of his union in
Ohio had experienced the closing of establishments belonging to
Motorola, Burroughs, Westinghouse, and General Electric. The
Ohio Association of Manufacturers, testifying in opposition to the
bill and on behalf of the business community, presented the myths
of big labor and of the business climate. They deemed the bill
anti-industry and anti-free enterprise and played on the fear that
the Community Readjustment Act would reduce private investment in the state. The bill died in the Commerce and Labor
Committee of the state senate at the end of 1978.[29]

The activities of OPIC generated interest beyond Ohio. Similar
coalitions were formed in other states and began to coordinate
their activities on a national basis. By 1979, 11 states (Connecticut,
Illinois, Maine, Massachusetts, Michigan, New York, New Jersey,
Oregon, Pennsylvania, Rhode Island, and Vermont) had similar
bills being considered in their state legislatures.

More Action at the Federal Level

The National Economic Efficiency Act of 1977 (NEEA) was
presented as an alternative to the National Employment Priorities

Act of 1974.[30] The NEEA required only one year's advance notice but put the burden of employee- and community-assistance fund payments on the employer rather than the government. It also eliminated the determination of justifiability, which had been so controversial in the NEPA. The NEEA was not passed.

In early 1978, Representatives Peter Kostmeyer (D–Penn.), Stanley Lundine (D–N.Y.), and Matthew McHugh (D–N.Y.) introduced the Voluntary Job Preservation and Community Stabilization Act into the House of Representatives.[31] This bill did not have a prenotification provision but was intended to enable interested employees or community groups to buy businesses in difficulty through technical and financial aid provided by the Department of Commerce. The bill also required the Secretary of Commerce to carry out investigations of local economies to identify enterprises in difficulty and threatened by potential dislocations.

These legislative events were accompanied by several important plant closings and massive layoffs that together seemed to assure the passage of some form of plant closing legislation. Between 1977 and 1979, the steel, automobile, and tire industries were racked by closings in Youngstown, Ohio (7500 steel workers laid off), Akron, Ohio (12,000 rubber workers), and Mahwah, New Jersey (11,000 auto workers). These closings and layoffs were joined by others in the same industries: 25 automobile plant closings, 24 rubber industry plant closings, and an 11% reduction in steel industry capacity. To these must be added the loss of employment indirectly linked to the major industrial closings. This indirect job loss among suppliers, subcontractors, local businesses dependent on the laid-off employees and local government is estimated at three to five times the direct job loss.[32]

Following these events and also the appearance of the Joint Union Study Tour recommendations discussed earlier, plant closing bills were reintroduced in Ohio, the eleven other states mentioned, and in the U.S. Senate and House of Representatives. The redrafted National Employment Priorities Act of 1979 was introduced in both houses of Congress on August 31, 1979 with 58 cosponsors including the entire Black Congressional Caucus.[33] Two similar bills were proposed in the Senate: the Employee Protection and Community Stabilization Act of 1979 was introduced by Harrison Williams (D–N.J.) and the other was introduced by Senator Howard Metzenbaum (D–Ohio).[34] Furthermore, amendments to bills dealing with the Economic

Development Administration and the Small Business Administration provided for financial and technical assistance to workers and communities interested in buying or establishing businesses that would preserve or create local employment.[35]

Senator Williams conducted hearings of the Labor and Human Resources Committee in several cities hard hit by plant closings— a practice that excited substantial public interest. The business press took a strong stand against the proposed legislation.[36] A quotation from *Industry Week* of February 4, 1980, is representative of this position:[37]

> *Business leaders clearly regard plant closing regulation as a priority threat. . . . The battle over plant closing controls may well set the tone of labor–management conflict in the new decade.*

The strong opposition of business interests bottled up the bills in committee until the 1980 election recess. The results of that election—bringing Ronald Reagan to the presidency, changing the composition of the Congress, and accentuating the conservative national tendencies—assured that the bills would die in committee. The arch-conservative, Orrin Hatch (R–Utah), replaced Senator Williams as chairman of the Labor and Human Resources Committee. Only 37 of the 64 senators and representatives who had sponsored plant closing bills remained in the Congress.

Between 1980 and 1982, two plant closing bills were introduced in Congress, including the updated National Employment Priorities Act of 1979. Nine more states introduced plant closing measures in their legislatures: Alaska, California, Delaware, Indiana, Iowa, Maryland, Minnesota, South Dakota and West Virginia.[38] California has instituted an executive task force to study the state's economy, locate potential closings, and coordinate aid or rescue efforts for closing or failing businesses and communities.[39]

To date, only 23 jurisdictions have considered plant closing bills and only eight have passed modest plant closing legislation. Of these eight, one (Wisconsin) has repealed the mandatory notice provisions, and another (Pittsburgh) has had its ordinance overturned in a state court. The Massachusetts and Connecticut bills mandate only the brief continuation of the health insurance of laid-off workers while making the notice provisions voluntary. Only the Vacaville (California), Philadelphia, Michigan, and Maine laws now require notice to government agencies. Only the Maine law requires notice to affected workers when a plant moves out of the state. In all of these laws, the notice period is only 60 days in advance of the closing, and the conditions under which notice is required are severely limited. Several states have created interagency task forces to provide information and technical assistance to businesses in difficulty and workers and communities affected by plant closings.[40]

A Closer Look at the State Level: The Case of Rhode Island

Initial Attempts at Legislation: The Friedemann Bill

Rhode Island is typical of the older industrial states suffering from plant closings and large-scale layoffs. In Rhode Island, as in other such states, the passage of plant closing legislation should have been easy. Plant closings and mass layoffs are frequent and the damage to workers' interests great. It is the most working-class state in the union. Only 11 other states have a higher percentage of unionized employees. The Democratic party, until 1984, had controlled both houses of the state legislature and, with a few exceptions, the governorship. Since the 1920s, Rhode Island has been the victim of three major waves of plant closings: first in the natural textile industry, then in the synthetic textile industry, and presently in the jewelry and heavy-electrical industries. Moreover, in 1973 two major military installations closed, causing a great loss of civilian employment.

During 1978 and 1979, 99 closings eliminated more than 4000 manufacturing jobs, and in 1980, the state lost 4600 jobs. During the first half of 1981, five important closings caused the loss of more than 1200 jobs. In 1982, the state lost 7000 manufacturing jobs. A recent study has set manufacturing job loss in Rhode Island due to closings, partial closings, and massive layoffs at over 40,000 during the period from 1972 to 1982. The majority of this job loss is attributed to the actions of corporations whose headquarters are not in Rhode Island.[41] The unemployment rate in recent years has frequently exceeded the national rate. These characteristics seem to signal the significant political presence of organized labor and the pressure of events favoring plant closing legislation.

The first plant closing bill was introduced in the General Assembly of Rhode Island in January of 1979 following the closing of several large plants.[42] The bill was drafted by an ad hoc committee representing unions, social service agencies, and community organizations and it was introduced by Representative Zygmunt Friedemann (D). The measure, modeled on the Ohio Community Readjustment Act, provided for two years' advance notice; a report on the effects and reasons of a closing; one week's severance pay for every year the employee had worked for the business; employer contributions to a Community Assistance Fund for aid to affected communities; and an Employee and Community Assistance Administration to enforce the provisions, administer the funds, and carry out economic studies, investigations of closings, and technical assistance projects.

Despite the support of Rhode Island locals of the United Automobile Workers, the United Steel Workers, the Amalgamated Clothing and Textile Workers, and the International Association of Machinists, the bill was not endorsed by the State Council of the AFL-CIO. Without the support of the State Council, the bill was assigned to the House Finance Committee. This led to its rapid extinction in committee.

The Mobilization of Forces: CLOC's Efforts

Despite this failure, the ad hoc committee continued its work in 1979 and several of the committee's most active members organized themselves under the title of the Community Labor Organizing Committee (CLOC). CLOC sought the support of union locals for antilayoff activities, particularly plant closing legislation. Because of the earlier failure and the more conservative political climate, CLOC was unable to find a single legislator willing to sponsor a comprehensive piece of legislation. Two measures less ambitious than the 1979 bill were introduced in the 1980 session. Senator Stephen Fortunato (D) introduced a bill providing for severance pay in case of a closing.[43] Representative Benjamin Lippitt (R) introduced a bill requiring notice four months prior to a closing.[44] Both bills were referred to the labor committees in their respective chambers, which found even the limited measures to be too ambitious.

During 1980, CLOC and several locals severely affected by closings and layoffs again sought support for a comprehensive plant closing bill. The coalition held a large meeting in March of 1980 where several state legislators and union leaders heard from victims of closings in Rhode Island and from coordinators of anti-plant closing campaigns in other states. Militant statements were made by rank and file unionists and by the heads of local unions affected by recent closings and layoffs. These statements were tinged with the bitterness that followed the discovery of the third face of power, the power of myth. They spoke of how they had accepted the necessity and good faith of their employers' actions, even though detrimental to the workers' interests, until they were abruptly laid off.

Silvio Santilli, President of Local 1542 of the IBEW, discussed the strike, sale, and closing of Narragansett Wire Company:[45]

> *The recent strike at Narrangansett Wire was a classic. They took everything out of the new contract—vacation, holidays, Christmas bonus, etc. The El Paso management announced they planned to liquidate. Then they sold ownership to the present management under a new name and said, "Take it or leave it!" Our people voted to ratify, saying that despite the union's recommendations, "[a]ny job's better than no job." So here we are back to square one, only 50 people back at work [out of 400], we're scraping the bottom of the barrel.*

In December of 1979 Coro/Richton Jewelry closed with one hour's notice to its employees. Winnie Carvalho, a 34-year veteran of the company, commented on how she and her 450 fellow workers were deceived:[46]

> *Before it closed, Coro had us working on imports. They didn't want anyone to know it. . . . Well [when we found out], we really didn't go to the union to fight for our rights. We didn't fight for our rights like we really should have.*

Although the legislators present were impressed by the information on closings and possible remedies, they were sceptical of the possibility of passing legislation in 1980 or 1981. They saw the business climate myth as having a very strong hold over the minds of their fellow legislators who were anxious to shed their reputation of being too favorable to labor. In spite of this scepticism, CLOC along with twelve local unions redrafted a bill, this time modeled on the NEPA of 1979. While advising against the proposal of such a comprehensive measure at that time, Representative Friedemann agreed to introduce the bill in the general assembly.

The proponents of the bill went to other unions and legislators for support. All the legislators advised that it had no chance of passage during that session. The bill received the support of the unions' rank and file, most notably in the unions hard hit by closings, but received neither leadership support nor the support of the State Council of the AFL-CIO. The State Council's position on important legislative issues was summed up by Ed McElroy, president of the Rhode Island AFL-CIO: "Labor's leadership views workers' compensation as the main area of concern."[47] The union's leadership had accepted the arguments of the business community that state plant closing legislation would hurt Rhode Island's business climate and would handicap the state in seeking new investment in competition with other states. Without much hope, the union leaders, and particularly the State Council, advocated national legislation and collective bargaining agreements to deal with plant closings.

Change of Tactics: A Working Compromise

In this unfavorable atmosphere, the supporters of state plant closing legislation were forced to change their tactics. When five state representatives proposed two limited bills instead of the comprehensive measure, the supporters of the comprehensive bill accepted the replacements and agreed to work for their passage. That decision was not easily made. Some of the supporting coalition members, particularly those from CLOC, argued that the limited bills would not generate enough enthusiasm among union activists to stimulate their lobbying efforts and that the threat of the more comprehensive legislation was needed in order to encourage fence-sitting legislators to support the limited bills. On the other hand, a majority of the CLOC membership supported the shift to the more limited bills as a foot-in-the-door for regulation that would be expanded in future legislative sessions.

The supporters of the limited bills directed their efforts toward gaining the endorsements of other labor and community organizations. They especially sought the endorsement of the Providence Federated Labor Council and the State Council of the AFL-CIO. On September 10, 1980, a spokesman for CLOC presented the Providence Labor Council with a resolution supporting the passage of state plant closing legislation including advance notice requirements, health benefit continuation, payments to affected workers and communities, and the investigation of closings by a state agency. The motion to adopt this resolution was amended from the floor to support only the general concept of federal plant closing legislation.

Meanwhile, advocates of state legislation were continuing to gain support of the state AFL-CIO through a resolution at the annual state labor convention in November. This resolution, the only resolution submitted by locals, was backed by 15 local unions. Despite efforts by state labor leaders to prevent the passage of any resolution favoring state plant closing legislation, the state convention did pass a resolution, much weaker than the one proposed by the locals, that supported the concept of state and federal legislation to require notification and assistance to workers threatened by a plant closing.

At the Legislative Council meeting of the state AFL-CIO in January of 1981, the state labor leaders agreed to come up with their own bill or support at least the health care continuation bill to be introduced the following month. The 1980 election had made it abundantly clear that there was no prospect for federal action on plant closings. Despite strong rank and file support for a more comprehensive state approach to plant closings, the state labor leadership still accepted the business climate argument. They were not particularly enthusiastic about endorsing the state health care continuation bill, but they felt pressured by rank and file demands for some action on plant closings.[48]

The Dominance of the Business Myth

On February 5, 1981, Democratic Representatives Friedemann, Teitz, Leven, McConnell, and Maigret introduced a bill requiring an employer to continue contributions for medical coverage for three months following the layoff of an employee.[49] On March 12, 1981, Teitz offered a bill specifying notice of four months prior to a closing or a substantial reduction of operations and envisioning the creation of a Board of Employee Readjustment to receive the notice, to investigate the effects of and reasons for the closing, and to coordinate job preservation efforts. The board was to have access to all records of the business.[50]

The committee hearings on the bills were scheduled for March 19 and 26, 1981, by which time the bills had garnered the endorsement of 20 unions and the support, though lukewarm, of the State Council of the AFL-CIO. At the first hearing, the Labor Committee heard only the witnesses in favor of the bills—12 labor representatives from textile, steel, electrical, and rubber unions,

Representative Friedemann, and a spokesperson for CLOC.

The opposition attended but did not speak. Nevertheless, resistance to the measure was manifested by several of the legislative
committee members in the form of hostile questioning of the
witnesses. The *Providence Journal* described the committee's
reaction in the following manner:[51]

> *House Labor Committee members were decidedly less enraptured*
> *[than those testifying in support] by Rep. Zygmunt J. Friedemann's*
> *proposed legislation, and they tossed skeptical questions at the legis-*
> *lator and the labor leaders.*

Without the necessity of testifying, the business community had
convinced the committee that plant closing legislation was bad
for Rhode Island despite the fact that eight of the thirteen committee members were Democrats and four were union members.
The business viewpoint was also that of Governor J. Joseph
Garrahy and his director of economic development. At the
second hearing, where the witnesses against the bills spoke, it was
evident that most present agreed with those who opposed the bill
even before they spoke. Three days after the second hearing, the
committee rejected the bills by a nine to four majority; five
Democrats and two union members voted against the bills.

The operation of the myth of big labor and the myth of the
business climate was highly visible in the attempt to pass the
health care continuation and advance bills. One member of the
legislative committee, himself a trade unionist, voted against the
bills, stating that they represented intrusions into matters that
"should be won at the bargaining table."[52] A worker who had
been forced to leave Rhode Island three years earlier due to the
loss of his job in a plant closing wrote a letter to the editor in the
Providence Journal, declaring that "it is exactly this type of legislation that is causing the mass exodus of companies from Rhode
Island."[53] Joseph Goodrich, Business Editor and columnist for the
Providence Journal-Bulletin, applauded the rejection of the notification as an important step in establishing a favorable business
climate in the state. Its passage would have meant "[t]hat management decision then would have been subject to an investigation
by a seven-member state board. . . ."[54]

The Final Chapter: The Greenhouse Commission

The maneuvering concerning plant closing legislation continued
in 1982. With its supporters continuing to press for the legislation

in the face of more closings and reductions in manufacturing operations, the Teitz bill was reintroduced on March 10, 1982, with the cosponsorship of Representatives Friedemann, Lippitt, Ferry, and Byrnes.[55] It was again referred to the House Labor Committee. This time the committee regarded the legislation more favorably in part because of strong constituent support and the menace of upcoming elections in which the coalition promised to campaign against Democrats from working-class districts who did not support the bill.

The supporters of the legislation organized meetings in the districts of each Democratic Labor Committee member. The turnout for the meetings in the working-class districts was large and vociferous. Four of the legislation's outspoken opponents of the previous year agreed to support the Teitz bill, and two agreed to become sponsors.

The euphoria that followed the favorable committee vote on this bill was short-lived. Before the full House could vote, Governor Garrahy threatened to veto the bill, reasoning that it would hurt the state's efforts to attract new business. An agreement was reached whereby a substitute bill was offered establishing the Plant Closing Study Commission to study plant closing regulation.[56] Supporters of the original bill would be well represented on the commission. This substitute bill was rapidly passed in both houses and became law without the governor's signature.

To counter the likely findings of this committee, the governor established the Greenhouse Commission, a task force to study economic development. The task force was heavily weighted in favor of business interests. As a result of this move and of the skillful management of publicity, the Plant Closing Study Commission was largely forgotten. For the next two years, the public's attention and the media were largely dominated by the governor's Greenhouse Commission. Although both the study committee and the task force concluded similarly that job preservation and the encouragement of local business were more important than the attraction of outside capital, the Greenhouse Commission early on voiced its disapproval of plant closing legislation and began to develop a complicated system of "positive" business incentives for the revitalization of Rhode Island's economy.

Despite this, state labor leaders were quick to support the Greenhouse plan as the best labor could hope for from the powerful business-oriented forces behind the plan. When the bond issue referendum for the support of the Greenhouse plan was defeated

in June 1984 by a vote of more than three to one, labor leaders
were left with having supported a plan that was seen by the voters
as a boondoggle for big business and the banks. The plan included
the elimination of unemployment benefits for striking workers
and the reduction of workers' compensation costs. These aspects
of the plan were the top priority of the business interests who
were primarily concerned with Rhode Island's business climate.
Because the labor members of the commission had agreed to
present the plan as a package and to support it without modifications, they were forced to publicly accept the business climate
arguments put forward for these changes. After the defeat of the
plan, changes in the unemployment compensation and workers'
comp laws were quickly passed in the legislature at the same time
that the mandate of the Plant Closing Commission was ter-
minated.[57]

The Business Climate Myth and the Failure
to Adopt Plant Closing Legislation

The political maneuvering in Rhode Island provides several
insights into the hidden faces of power and the uses of the myths
of big labor and of the business climate. The initiatives of those
who supported plant closing legislation were greeted with suspicion by labor leaders who had already begun to accept the business climate arguments. At this point, the sweep of the legislation
was substantially diminished in anticipation of the force of the
business opposition. Even though labor leaders were finally
prodded into supporting the less comprehensive legislation, the
myths retained their influence over the legislators even with little
opposing testimony from business representatives. When con-
certed efforts by backers of the legislation pushed the bills
through the Labor Committee, business forces mustered substantial support from the governor and killed the legislation. A study
commission was formed instead, which, in turn, was undermined
by the creation of the Greenhouse Commission.

It was agreed that 3 out of 12 members of the Greenhouse
Commission would be labor leaders. The labor leaders were
interested in this commission rather than the Plant Closing Study
Commission because the former had as members the most promi-
nent business leaders in the state. It was clear from the start which

commission would have the ears of the governor and the legislators.

In reaching agreement on the Greenhouse plan, the labor leaders made significant concessions in their original demands. There
were no provisions in the plan to assure union or worker representation in the businesses that received state money. While
moneys were earmarked for job creation, no payback or sanctions were to be imposed on businesses that received funds but
did not create the promised jobs or dismissed workers the
moment the government funding ceased. Firms that were engaging in unfair labor practices and union-busting were not to be
excluded from receiving funds nor were firms which intended to
use the money to hire new workers during a strike. Affirmative
action requirements other than those already a part of state and
federal law were not included in the plan.

After the labor leaders had made their concessions and had
agreed to support the plan as a package, the issues of strikers'
unemployment benefits and workers' compensation cost reduction were raised. These had not been part of prior discussions.
The business leaders argued that their constituency, Rhode Island
business, was primarily concerned with improving the state's
business climate. They could not return to that constituency with
a plan that did not include the repeal of strikers' benefits and the
reduction of workers' compensation costs. The strength of the
business climate myth is indicated by the fact that this contention
came after substantial research had been presented to the commission demonstrating that the existing laws were not, in fact,
more costly to businesses than those in other states. In particular,
the research showed that the strikers' benefits provisions had cost
the state and employers very little and that it had had no measur-
able effect on the duration of strikes. Nevertheless, labor leaders
had little choice other than scrapping the entire plan and having
nothing to show for their efforts, so they accepted the business
leaders' additions to the plan.[58]

This treatment of the political history of plant closing legislation nationally and in one particular state is a demonstration of the
power of business interests both in the direct and open political
give-and-take of lobbying and over the minds of decision makers,
the public, and even the victims of plant closings. The myths of
big labor and of the business climate were adopted by legislatures
in spite of the facts that public hearings seemed to be dominated

by the proponents of plant closing legislation and that the few business representatives who were present mustered little or no data, relying primarily on the emotive force of the myths.

Rhode Island was no exception. In December 1979, the New York general assembly, for example, rejected plant closing legislation after several days of public hearings. In those hearings only three persons testified against the proposed legislation. Characteristic of that testimony and of the testimony against such legislation in other federal and state hearings was the testimony of William Delevan, Chairman of the State/Federal Legislative Committee of the Greater Syracuse Chamber of Commerce. Delevan complained:[59]

> *This legislation seeks to tear down a fundamental division between public and private sectors that has existed for well over 200 years in our nation's history. With this legislation the state will be directly stepping into the rightful domain of private sector decision-making. . . .*
>
> *What this legislation would do would be to punish businesses for exercising a basic instinct—financial survival. First, while a business is already overtaxed and overregulated, this legislation would add additional payroll expenses setting up a cushion fund for severance pay. And then it would restrict the business' [sic] inherent right to decide what is best for his or her business by requiring one-year notification. And, finally, it would require a so-called economic impact statement which will be reviewed no less by the very bureaucratic state which has created the overloaded regulations in the first place. In addition, this legislation will seriously jeopardize the equal party status at the negotiating table. Right now, when labor demands become excessive, management retains the option of temporarily or permanently closing plants. . . . Now, management would have to give one-year notice, a requirement which leaves management completely at the mercy of labor at the bargaining table.*

Similarly, the chairperson of the Congressional Action Committee of the South Jersey Chamber of Commerce called attempts to pass federal plant closing legislation misguided because[60]

> *[c]ompanies that close a plant or move a plant do so for various reasons usually of an economic nature.*
>
> *This proposed legislation misses the basic illness and tries to treat the symptoms while impairing management's ability to make necessary decisions which improve its economic position and provide future jobs.*

Democratic politicians, who style themselves as prolabor, from states hard hit by closings and layoffs have accepted the "business climate" argument. Governor William O'Neill of Connecticut, for example, has "opposed any requirement that companies give advance notice because it would send a signal that Connecticut was 'antibusiness.'"[61] To the extent that politicians, the public, and even workers themselves accept the position that management prerogatives are inviolable even in the face of substantial evidence of management's failure to preserve community viability and employment, the business climate myth is a powerful tool to maintain power without accountability to any but business interests.

Job security has now become a top priority for organized labor. Concessions on wages and work rules have been given in return for minimal guarantees. These guarantees generally apply to limiting some previously planned closing or layoffs. Only in three instances have companies agreed to give unions advance notice and the opportunity to negotiate over future total or partial closings.[62] Here again the crucial play of all three faces of power is evident. In the 1970s, labor leadership's perception of its bargaining power and its acceptance of business arguments for the need to reduce labor militancy precluded strong support of plant closing legislation. This was particularly true at the local level where the most militant unionists, in coordination with community groups, were fighting for such legislation. Furthermore, the acceptance of the probusiness myths also precluded a tough negotiating position on job security.

After 1982, when labor turned its attention to these issues, it found that its strength was not adequate to wrest solid job guarantees and protections against layoffs and closings from business. It found as well that politicians, both local and national, had accepted the incontrovertability of the argument that capital mobility must be unfettered in order to provide an attractive "business climate" and that the reduction of labor's "excessive" power was prerequisite to improving the business climate.[63]

The Power of the Myth of Big Labor

Origins of the Myth

The myth of big labor—or the belief that organized labor is excessively powerful and a handicap to effective business deci-

sion making—is not of recent origin. It has been a part of the
ideology of American business since the inception of trade unionism, and it has become particularly strong in the postwar era. In
1948, Charles Wilson, then president of General Motors,
warned:[64]

> *If we consider the ultimate result of this tendency to stretch collective
> bargaining to comprehend any subject that a union leader may desire
> to bargain on, we come out with the union leaders really running the
> economy of the country. . . . Under these conditions, the freedom of
> management to function properly without interference in making its
> everyday decisions will be gradually restricted. The Union leaders—
> particularly where they have industry-wide power—will have the
> deciding vote in all managerial decisions, or at least, will exercise a
> veto power that will stop progress. . . . Competition will be stifled
> and progress in the improvement of industrial processes which
> reduce the cost and price of goods produced by industry will be
> halted.*

The real force of the myth is revealed by the fact that the public
and trade unionists themselves have come to accept Wilson's
view of the labor movement. "We are victims of our own success," says a Rhode Island bricklayers' union official.[65] How did
the myth of big labor develop and gain such acceptance? There
are at least three sources.

First, the myth was closest to being true during the rapid
industrial unionization between 1935 and 1945 when union membership increased from 3.7 million to 14.7 million in spite of
strong resistance from employers. The militancy of the Congress
of Industrial Organizations (CIO) and its success in making
industrial unions a visible force in the corridors of power did have
mythic proportions.

Second, the myth rested on the growing frequency of collective bargaining during the 1940s and 1950s and the massive
strikes, particularly in steel and the mines, during that period.
While strike settlements and collective bargaining in general
became progressively more limited to compensation and benefit
issues, bargaining was presented to the public as the preferred
form of "industrial democracy."[66]

Beginning in 1950, more and more union contracts contained
no-strike clauses, barring a major tool for resolving grievances
and sapping labor militancy. The formal and hierarchical grievance procedures that replaced more militant labor actions for

dealing with grievances moved these issues quickly away from the shop floor and the immediate control of the rank and file. Collective bargaining did result in a major increase in industrial wages in oligopolistic industries such as autos, steel, chemicals, and rubber but the wage increases never exceeded a fractional share of productivity and price increases. Furthermore, in large part due to structural, economic, and demographic changes such as the relative decline of farmers and the self-employed and increase of employees, the share of national income going to workers increased dramatically. This effect was often attributed to union strength and collective bargaining.

A third source of the myth is the harmful publicity during the 1940s and 1950s stemming from Cold War anti-Communist hysteria and McCarthyism. The labor movement itself participated in this by purging the left-wing leaders and unions from the CIO. The bad press persisted during the Senate antiracketeering hearings of the 1950s, resulting again in the widely publicized ouster of the Teamster's Union from the AFL-CIO and the fixing of the image of Jimmy Hoffa as the powerful union boss. In the 1960s and 1970s the labor movement lost the respect of liberal opinion because of the widely publicized resistance of some unions to the civil rights, environmental, and antiwar movements. The media focus on the putative role of union wage and benefit demands in the cost-push inflation of the 1970s and 1980s seemed to exclude other explanations for inflation. The media, even when hostile to organized labor, stressed the economic power and political influence of the labor movement.

Realities Behind the Myth

The myth conceals harsh realities. Without the cooperation or at least the disinterest of the business community, organized labor has little political clout. Anthony Mazzocchi of the Oil, Chemical, and Atomic Workers Union has suggested that the rapid unionization between 1935 and 1945 was the first and last great victory of the American labor movement. This success was fostered by the government and the Wagner Act of 1935. Since that time, the bargaining power and the political power of unions have undergone a steady decline which has recently become precipitous.[67]

The courts have generally acted to restrict the growth of labor union power. In one of its earliest decisions on the NLRA, *NLRB v. Mackay Radio Telegraph Co.*, the U.S. Supreme Court established a tradition of relying on the nineteenth century employment relation to interpret the act.[68] The Court construed the act in such a way as to preclude on the side of labor all collective actions not specifically authorized in the act while granting to management, as the representative of capital, all actions not specifically prohibited.[69] This tradition has been maintained even by liberal justices such as William O. Douglas and William J. Brennan.

In *Boys Markets, Inc. v. Retail Clerks Local 770*, the Court granted management's request for an injunction against a strike based on an acknowledged employee grievance because there were other contractual means for trying to settle the grievance.[70] The maintenance of "industrial peace," too often a code phrase for continuing production at the expense of labor's demands, has superseded the NLRA's Section 13 prohibition of interfering with the right to strike and the avowed congressional intent of ending the use of the hated labor injunction.

Since 1947, the legislative agenda of organized labor has met with little success. The Taft–Hartley Amendments of 1947, passed over union opposition, created a category of unfair labor practices directed at union activities, prohibited the negotiation of closed-shop agreements, and authorized the states to prohibit the negotiation of union shop agreements. (Twenty states, principally in the South and West, have since taken advantage of the latter provision.) The Taft–Hartley Amendments were the legislative response to the massive strikes of 1946 in all major industries to demand work rule changes and large wage increases after the freeze on wages during the Second World War. While the workers received substantial wage increases, they were forced to drop their demands for inroads into managerial prerogatives. Labor's militancy and these participatory demands were severely penalized by the Taft–Hartley Amendments and successive governmental investigations into the activities of left-wing labor militants.

After a decade of legislative hearings, purges of union leaders, and a major steel strike, Congress again responded with legislation hostile to the unions. The Landrum–Griffin Act of 1959 imposed restrictions on the choice of union officials and imposed financial reporting requirements on all union activities. The act also created mechanisms for the governmental intervention in and the prohibition of strikes and limited the tactics available to unions in actions against employers.

The labor movement achieved partial and fragile successes only in legislation providing minimum standards of protection for workers from job loss due to foreign competition (Trade Adjustment Act of 1962 and Foreign Trade Act of 1974), from occupational health and safety hazards (Occupational Health and Safety Act of 1970), and from loss of pension benefits (Employee Retirement Income Security Act of 1974).[71] Organized labor has not been able to secure the principal items of its legislative agenda—the revocation of the closed-shop prohibition, the prohibition of state interference with union shop agreements, the restriction of union busting activities, and the protection of common-situs picketing.[72]

In addition to legislative failures, several other indicators have signaled the contrary reality behind the myth of union power. The proportion of workers unionized has fallen from a peak of 25% in 1953 to less than 18% in 1983. Between 1960 and 1976 the percentage of blue-collar workers protected by collective bargaining agreements in metropolitan areas decreased 12 points while the percentage of white-collar metropolitan workers protected by such agreements declined 4 points. The percentage of certification elections won by unions has decreased from 81% in 1947 to less than 40% in 1983. Decertifications have climbed from 300 cases per year in 1970 to over 1000 in 1983.[73]

A look at recent changes in worker income provides another indication of the myth. The hourly wage of manufacturing workers only increased, in 1967 dollars, 7.8% between 1967 and 1979. In that same period, the gross national product increased 43% and reported corporate profits increased 37% (both also in 1967 dollars). Since 1979, production workers have suffered a decline in the real spendable hourly wage. Hourly wages and labor costs of the American labor force have grown more slowly since 1960 than those of other Western industrialized countries (including Japan). The 1984 round of industrial contract negotiations resulted in wage increases substantially below the rate of inflation. Furthermore, the United States has generally had an unemployment rate higher than that of the OECD countries (except Canada).[74]

The myth of big labor hides facts that are evident when the power of labor in actual confrontations with employers is analyzed. In the 1970 auto workers strike against General Motors, the UAW's seemingly massive war chest was exhausted in a few months, although strikers' families never received more than $25

per month. In the unsuccessful attempt by the United Steel
Workers to organize Du Pont, Du Pont was able to outstaff the
USWA campaign by 50 to 1. When the oil, chemical, and atomic
workers struck against Shell Oil for 364 days, they were able to
prevent replacement workers from being hired—yet, they were
unable to stop one drop of oil from being refined. One third of
Shell's employees are supervisors an important part of whose role
is to maintain production during labor disputes. The real power
of public employees' unions, usually barred by law from striking,
was clearly demonstrated in the destruction of the Professional
Air Traffic Controllers Organization (PATCO).[75]

The myth of big labor has veiled several important facts about
the labor movement and its role in the nation's political and
economic life. It has clouded the facts that only a small and
declining proportion of workers are union members, that the
economic gains of union workers have been only a fraction of the
productivity gains and the increased profits they have produced,
that trade unions cannot be blamed for cost-push inflation, and
that the legislative agenda of organized labor has not been readily
adopted. The acceptance of the myth of big labor results in a
drastic distortion of the public debate on who is responsible for
economic difficulties and who should bear the brunt of the sacri-
fices to resolve these difficulties.

Acceptance of the Myth

The myth of big labor has been so well accepted because it plays
to widespread interests and feelings. It is evident that the myth is
valuable to business interests. It, along with the related myth of
the business climate, furnishes a public justification for the efforts
of business and government to reduce the power of unions and to
oppose the demands of workers. It helps to implicate union
leadership in the efforts to curb spontaneous rank and file job
actions and wildcat strikes. Moreover, the myth gives employers
and management an excuse for their own failures.

The attraction of the myth to unions and workers is less evident; nevertheless, the attraction exists. The myth gives union
workers a kind of dignity, importance, and hope in their confrontations with the realities of the powerlessness in their daily work
life. If work diminishes the worker's self-esteem more and more,
belonging to a powerful union makes him seem more significant.
If a worker has in reality lost more and more control over her job

situation, a powerful union gives her hope of the negotiated improvement of her position. Finally, the myth functions to the advantage of union leaders in raising their social status and in maintaining their authority over their rank and file.

The major reason for the acceptance of the myth of big labor in its most negative form is that the economic dominance of business over labor is translated into the dominance of probusiness, and antiunion, ideas. One aspect of this that William Winpisinger, head of the International Association of Machinists, has often cited is the annual figures for lobbying: $3 million for the unions and $2 billion for business. The same disparity is apparent in election contributions, particularly since the removal of many restrictions on political action committees.

The political and economic dominance of business allows it to monopolize the images conveyed to the public (including workers) by the media. For example, during the attempt to organize Du Pont, the USWA prepared radio and television messages concerning the benefits of trade unionism and USWA representation. The union was refused access to the media by station managers fearing that they would have to provide equal time for the company and independent unions to air their positions. Meanwhile, Du Pont was running product advertisements, displaying the company name before the public and its workers.[76]

A good example of hidden ways in which the third face of power works comes from Rhode Island. Peter Gosselin, the labor reporter for the *Providence Journal–Bulletin*, considers himself to be to the left-of-center and prolabor. In lamenting the criticism that Rhode Island's only statewide daily paper and his reporting gets from labor, he discounts the influence of Henry Sharpe, corporate officer of both Brown & Sharpe Manufacturing and of the *Journal–Bulletin*, and of the clearly antilabor editorial policy of the paper. He states flatly that "I've never been told what angle to take on a labor issue." At the same time, he notes that the paper only gives him two days per week to cover labor while it covers business in several pages each day. "I have to skip an awful lot of nuts and bolts stories that I should be covering," Gosselin admits.[77]

The positive aspects of unions are generally absent from the media. Few TV dramas or films deal with unions at all, and union commercials are rare. When unions make the news, it is generally for a labor dispute or because of corruption. While business ideas are pervasive in schools at all levels, unions are rarely, if ever, mentioned. The effect of this is evident. In a study commissioned by the AFL-CIO of the attitudes of nonunion workers, 65% believed that "unions force members to go along with decisions they don't like"; 54% believe that "unions increase the risk that companies will go out of business"; and 57% believed that "unions stifle individual initiative."[78]

Again the Rhode Island Greenhouse Plan referendum provides additional data indicating the influence of employers' ideas even over union members. Although the plan was strongly supported by the state's trade unions, members of union households were no more likely to vote for it than members of nonunion households. However, two-thirds of employees who thought that their employer supported the plan voted for it and 86% of those who thought their employer was against the plan voted against it.[79]

The historical context of the early growth in union membership is also an important element of the explanation. The industrial unions were dramatically successful in organizing at the height of the depression—when unemployment was at extremely high levels, when a major portion of industrial productive capacity was idle, and when wages were very low. The newly organized unions aimed at protecting existing jobs and at obtaining a wage scale adequate for a decent life.

As with most myths, there was a kernel of truth to the myth of big labor that gripped the public imagination. The rekindling of the economy immediately prior to and during the entry into WW II was astonishing. Unemployment fell rapidly and at the same time employers offered workers, now in demand, a softening of their resistance to higher salaries—provided that the unions did not challenge management prerogatives and the growth of production. The government encouraged the cooperation between workers and employers by its appeals to patriotism and its stimulation of the economy.

After the war, the government continued its policy of economic stimulation in order to maintain a high level of economic growth and to absorb the returning veterans. All of this was linked in the public mind with the aggressive organizing campaigns of the 1930s, the tripling of union membership between 1935 and 1945, the alliance of business, unions, and government during the war, and the major strikes following the war. The wartime and postwar economic scene seemed to be dominated by a triple alliance of big government, big business, and big labor.

The Power of the Myths of the Business Climate and Legality

The myth of the business climate and the myth of legality also developed their influence on American labor relations and labor politics in the period between the height of the depression and the end of World War II. Three attitudes flowed from labor's experience during and immediately after the war, and as with all infants, the experience of the formative years had a profound effect on later development. First was the confidence that rapid economic growth would lead to a continuous increase of employment and of wages. Second was the faith that private enterprise was the motor of economic development, thus relegating government to the significant, but secondary, role of stimulating business growth and productivity and of promoting collective bargaining in a framework of cooperation.

These attitudes have encouraged unions to contest only the extent of their share in the profits of economic growth, not the wisdom or methods of achieving growth. Unions have linked their wage demands to a small share of the profits from increased business productivity. After having done that, they are in a bad position to resist layoffs, automation, and taylorism or speed-ups in the name of improved productivity.

The third attitude was an overriding respect for legality and administrative processes. Many workers saw, not without some justification, the New Deal labor legislation, rather than their own militant actions, as the basis for the growth of trade unions and the unionized workers' share in economic growth. These workers were hard-pressed to reject the legal processes by which their new rights were interpreted and limited in the light of preexisting notions of "managerial prerogative."

As with most rights achieved through difficult struggles, often requiring illegal acts, they tend to be rescinded or restricted when the struggle ebbs or takes on more easily controlled and co-optive forms. Formal grievance procedures and the National Labor Relations Board's (NLRB) complaint procedure were important gains for the labor movement. As the grievance procedures became more routine, formal, and hierarchical and as the NLRB became an arena for experts to tie issues up in procedural maneuvers, respect for the legally mandated procedures tended to sap local initiative and rank and file militancy. Disputes were constantly referred to "higher authorities" and their resolution became more and more remote from the shop floor and the daily concerns of workers. Losing their roots and their energy, with directly concerned workers frustrated by delay and attrition, the disputes were easily negotiated away, between top management and union leaders, and in an atmosphere of cooperation that belies the importance of the issues to the individuals involved at the local level.

To accept the myth of legality has two consequences, both detrimental to the power of workers. The first consequence is that grievances that are not recognized by existing legal procedures or are resolved against the workers are seen as illegitimate (i.e., the existing legal procedures are seen as the final arbiter of the justice or injustice of the workers' claim). Other, possibly more effective, means of resolving the grievances may be ignored because they do not comport with the established legal framework. This is to forget the purpose and intensity of the struggles in which these procedures originated. The purpose of the struggles was not simply to establish legal procedures, but to establish procedures that would be effective and expedient in protecting workers' rights *as determined by the workers' notions of justice.* The struggles were intense and generally required engaging in acts that were illegal at the time and which, while possibly still illegal, may again be necessary to establish and protect workers' rights.

The second consequence is that confusion and bitterness result when the legal procedures are remote, slow, and burdensome but are allowed to channel the grievances of the workers. The bitterness is often directed at the union, which is seen as standing behind the ineffective legal remedies. The confusion leaves workers at a loss as to how to resolve their grievances in a way that conforms to their sense of justice. This is disastrous for a labor movement facing determined employers in a time of economic crisis. The labor movement needs determined and united workers who see the movement as securing justice for workers.[80]

Effects of the Myths on the Postwar Labor Movement

The primary effect of the myths of big labor, of the business climate, and of legality in the postwar period has been to foster close, but asymmetric, cooperation between labor leaders and business interests. The cooperation is asymmetric because, while

organized workers realized important gains in wages and benefits, the labor movement gave away opportunities to enhance its
solidarity and political power. Ultimately, this endangered wages
and benefits as well.

Two examples of this cooperation and its negative effects on
employment and union strength are illustrative. John L. Lewis,
former chief of the mine workers and himself one of the heroes of
the labor movement in the 1930s, cooperated in the mechaniza-
tion of the mines to the point of loaning money from the workers'
pension fund to mine owners for the purchase and installation of
machinery. In doing this, Lewis was accepting the loss of large
numbers of jobs and union members in order to obtain substantial
wage increases for those who remained in the mines. The second
example leads into the present wave of plant closings and high
unemployment. After the accords that ended the massive strikes
of 1946 and which substantially augmented industrial wages after
a period of blockage, the principal industries (notably steel, automobile, petroleum, textile, and tire) raised their prices to a level
unjustified by the wage increases. In a conspiracy of silence, the
unions failed to contest the blaming of the entire price increase on
the wage increases.

This practice has continued. Since 1946, the oligopolistic industries (automobile, steel, chemical, and heavy electrical) have
traditionally blamed wage increases for price increases that are
200 to 300% greater than wage increases. Satisfied with the wage
increases, trade unions have not protested these price increases.[81]
This process has greatly weakened public support for union
demands and for collective bargaining and has reinforced the
notion of the wage–price spiral. Furthermore, by allowing the
one-time oligopolistic industries to engage in administering prices
with impunity, the unions have allowed these industries to lose
their ability to compete in a no longer oligopolistic world market.
The support of unions such as the United Steel Workers for the
companies' calls for import limitations continues this trend. All of
these developments have led to loss of jobs and wage concessions.

The asymmetry of cooperation has hurt the ability of the labor
movement to achieve its goals through collective bargaining.
Since 1945, business has greatly changed its structure, has developed expertise in all of the social sciences in order to better
manage its work force, and has operated internationally. The
horizontal and vertical integration of conglomerates endows

them with the capacity to transfer quickly their capital and their production processes. The labor movement has not developed the means for challenging that capacity.

Another imbalance lies in the labor movement's inability to match the expertise that business gleans from business, engineering, and law schools oriented toward the needs of business. Finally, unions have not developed the capacity to act internationally in the face of challenges from multinational enterprises and consortia.

These asymmetries mean that cooperation is the agreement or adherence of unions to the decisions of management in exchange for wage and benefit increases. Such cooperation has so increased the power of management relative to that of the unions that the latter must now accept, in addition, wage and benefit freezes or reductions.

The myths and their consequences have severely constricted the labor movement. Because of the position to which the movement has relegated the government, labor cannot easily demand the direct intervention of government in the management of business enterprises. Thus, the movement is not in a position to accord a high priority to bills requiring advance notice of closings or government intervention in management disinvestment decisions. Since unions have accepted management prerogatives as a precondition for cooperation, they are unprepared to demand their own participation in investment decisions that will ultimately determine levels and conditions of employment. By placing their orientation on dividing up increases of productivity, unions have been forced to place unemployment, which sometimes leads to productivity increases, outside of the framework of collective bargaining. The unemployed are relegated to government programs which only furnish temporary aid because, from the mythic perspective, in a growing economy unemployment is always temporary.

This misconception that unemployment is always temporary reflects another dangerous constriction of the labor movement that is related to the myths of big labor, of the business climate, and of legality. The labor movement has shown a similar attitude toward all the groups that, like the unemployed, have been outside the mainstream of industrial employment—blacks, women, agricultural workers, students, and the hard-core poor. The labor movement has too often distanced itself from political and social developments essential to building a solid base for worker power. Unions have cut themselves off from some of the most dynamic movements of recent years—the civil rights movement, feminism, the antiwar movement, the welfare rights movement, and environmentalism. Similarly, the labor movement has not reacted quickly enough or adequately to the restructuring of employment toward the tertiary sector. This slow reaction has been aggravated by the movement's uncertain concern for the needs of blacks, women, and the unemployed who have moved into the tertiary sector jobs.

Summary and Preliminary Conclusions

In this chapter, we have established the importance of and begun to answer the questions raised in Chapter 1. Evidence has been presented to document the dire straits of many workers, trade unions, and communities that have been the victims of plant closings and large-scale layoffs. The evidence leads to the conclusion that regulation and control of plant closings and layoffs is in the interest of both workers and trade unions. Such regulation and control does not presently exist to any extent in this country. Furthermore, widespread or substantial income or reemployment guarantees are not available to displaced workers from government, voluntary employers' plans, or collective bargaining agreements.

Given this state of affairs, it would seem reasonable and predictable that workers and organized labor would unite solidly and energetically behind proposed plant closing legislation. This, as the evidence presented showed, has rarely been the case. Only the most militant trade unionists, allied with community groups representing the unemployed and other disadvantaged groups, have given their wholehearted support to such legislation. Even where major unions have supported the legislation their efforts have generally been unsuccessful in countering the opposition of business interests. An especially interesting aspect of this situation is the apparent lack of need for strong business lobbying against the legislation, at least in public hearings. The public, legislators, and many trade unionists seem to accept the business position against plant closing legislation with little need for supporting evidence.

The hidden faces of power have been presented as a preliminary explanation for the seeming ease with which plant closing
legislation has gone down to defeat despite its strong interest for
workers and the minimal opposition heard at public hearings. The
hidden faces of power—in the form of the myths of big labor, of
the business climate, and of legality—act behind the scenes to shape
the agenda and the views of participants in the decision-making
processes. Despite the clear weight of the evidence, the public,
officials, workers, and even trade unionists begin to accept the
view that labor's power is excessive and that it places unnecessary
burdens on business detrimental to its competitiveness. They
come to believe (again despite the evidence) that any regulation of
business activities in favor of workers damages the ability of a city,
state, or nation to attract business investment. They adopt the
position that existing legal remedies are adequate to resolve justly
workers' grievances and that grievances not resolved by existing
procedures are not legitimate. Given the widespread acceptance
of these myths, plant closing legislation is not the order of the day.

We have traced the growth and acceptance of these myths
through the depression, World War II, and the postwar period.
They gather support from the rapid unionization under the auspi-
ces of the NLRA and in the cooperation between business, labor,
and government during the war. The early postwar period of
economic growth, punctuated occasionally by large and well-
publicized strikes, was characterized by the acquiescence of
labor in business decisions in exchange for a share of productivity
increases in the form of higher wages and benefits. The media
have played an important role in perpetuating the myth of big
labor by tending to give only sporadic coverage to labor issues and
then primarily to strikes, corruption, and large wage settlements.

Strategies and Recommendations

The foregoing analysis of the American case studies suggests that
workers and their unions face formidable obstacles when they
attempt to protect their jobs, their livelihoods, and their communities from plant closings and economic dislocation. The economic
and political power of business interests which support the unfettered mobility of capital is great. That power is bolstered by
myths that are not supported by evidence but, nevertheless, have

a strong psychological hold on the public, government officials, and even workers themselves. The power of workers and trade unions is further reduced because they have not been able to build strong alliances with other groups challenging the same or similar myths that support the dominance of business interests.

Although additional evidence will come in later chapters from the comparison of the American and the French cases, several preliminary suggestions at this point can be drawn. These suggestions are based on the analysis of the role of the myths of big labor, of the business climate, and of legality in the failure of plant closing legislation in the United States. This analysis points toward a radical program for the labor movement. The recommendations come under three headings: (1) increasing worker militancy, (2) increasing unionization and solidarity, and (3) developing political unionism.

The recommendations are directed to trade unions, not for the purpose of "blaming the victim," but because the labor movement is the only organized and widely accepted representative of American workers. The protection of workers' jobs and livelihoods and the health of the labor movement make moving in these directions imperative. At the present, however, it cannot be assumed that the recommendations will be easy or even possible to implement.[82]

Worker Militancy

To the extent that worker militancy has been sapped by the routinization and legalization of disputes, increasing militancy requires that less attention be paid to the legal and traditional forms of asserting workers' claims. In particular, the threat of plant closings and large-scale layoffs cannot be countered effectively by arbitration, NLRB complaints, or even by traditional strikes. Other tactics such as occupations, boycotts, mass demonstrations, temporary work stoppages, strikes, and job actions against all of a company's facilities and affiliates must be used more regularly. New and effective tactics must be developed to meet the threat to workers, whether or not those tactics conform to the letter of the law. By taking the initiative in developing new tactics, the labor movement will have the delay from the backlog at the NLRB working in their favor rather than in the favor of employers.

Locals must be encouraged to support the initiatives of their more militant members, and union headquarters must support their most militant locals. Unions must consider supporting non-members and other organizations that are taking action against those businesses with whom the unions also have a dispute. In the case of plant closings, all levels of the trade union movement should encourage and aid local takeovers, buyouts, cooperatives, and public enterprises to own and operate the threatened facilities.

Two traditional provisions of collective bargaining agreements are obsolete and should be eliminated. The "no-strike" and "managerial prerogative" provisions routinely included in union contracts function to prevent workers from challenging the investment and operating decisions that must ultimately determine job security, working conditions, wages, and benefits. While workers must have access to an effective grievance procedure and ultimately arbitration to handle many routine disputes, major managerial decisions affecting many workers' jobs and livelihoods cannot await a drawn-out arbitration or the expiration of the contract. Such delays sap militancy and defuse resistance. Management decisions, or indecision, detrimental to important interests of many workers must be met by stiff and swift collective resistance.

When the proven economic difficulties of a business require concession bargaining, the concessions must be mutual. Any reduction in wage and benefit demands or changes in work rules required to aid the business must be counterbalanced by a reduction in the scope of managerial prerogatives, by increased worker access to corporate information, by increased participation of workers in management decisions, and by increased job security. In this way, an attempt can be made to turn the economic hardship of the business, which should be a bargaining disadvantage, to the long-term advantage of the workers.

Unionization and Solidarity

Increased worker militancy does not arise in a vacuum. It must be based on widespread and effective organization, a strong sense of solidarity, and community support. Unions must, of course, keep up their organizing efforts. These efforts should be coupled with a new outlook on organizational solidarity. Trade union membership must no longer be seen as a necessary evil or a burden, occasionally useful for protecting a worker against an overbearing employer. Trade unionism must be seen as a lifetime commitment to bettering the lives of past, present, and future workers.

On the negative side, this means that unions cannot negotiate tiered compensation systems that discriminate against the newly hired, the retired, or the about to be retired. On the positive side, American unions (like their European counterparts) should provide their members with a greater array of services—cultural and social events; educational and study programs (not simply job- and union-related matters); social, medical, and legal services; vacation colonies and tours; representation of workers' broader interests outside the workplace before governmental agencies; and housing assistance. These activities bind existing members more closely together and to their unions and provide incentives for nonmembers to join the union.

The unemployed and the retired must retain their union membership and have an impact on union activities. The union must play a strong role in improving their benefits, status, and opportunities. In the context of plant closings and large layoffs, the retention of union status for those no longer employed can help to sustain resistance. Furthermore, unions should actively organize the retired and unemployed who were not previously union members.

With the large increase of jobs in office and service work, special efforts must be made to discover and serve the needs of workers in these fields. Many of these jobs are held by women, ethnic minorities, and the previously unemployed. These workers may be especially interested in equal opportunity and comparable worth, day-care, respectful treatment, part-time employment, job advancement and training, job security, and flexible work schedules. New forms of union-linked associations should be created for nonmembers in order to provide them services, educate them in the advantages of full membership, and give them a chance to inform the unions of what their needs are. Special attention should be paid to ways of encouraging the family members of trade unionists to play a more active role in the union.

Internal solidarity and attractiveness to nonmembers require that unions increase their attention to individual workers and their problems—on the shop floor and elsewhere. This would be facilitated by a revival of the steward structure and a greater role for stewards in union decision making at all levels. Coupled with this emphasis on stewards, who are chosen by and identify most closely with their coworkers at the shop level, must be a reidentification of union leaders with the rank and file. Union leaders are often criticized for the fact or appearance of being too close to management. This image, which gives credence to the myth of big labor, is bolstered by high salaries, sumptuous offices, and perks that resemble those of executives for large businesses. Union leaders should have substantial rank and file experience in the trade or industry with which they deal. They should avoid anything that lessens their identification with their members. There should be a greater reliance on volunteers from the rank and file to fill important leadership positions. The volunteers would be compensated for their actual out-of-pocket expenses or their loss of wages during an unpaid full or partial leave of absence from their regular employment.

Political Unionism

The failures to pass plant closing legislation were political failures. The importance of the myths of big labor, the business climate, and legality are found in their political effects. These must be countered by more conscious and militant labor politics. Trade unions are politically active. In the 1984 presidential election campaign, the AFL-CIO took an unprecedented political step in endorsing a Democratic candidate in the primaries. The link between labor and Walter Mondale turned out to be a liability for both parties in that it tended to reinforce the myth of big labor and suggest that the election of the Democratic candidate would be detrimental to the business climate.

In addition to their traditional political activities of supporting prolabor candidates and lobbying for legislation directly addressing labor–management relations, the labor movement must attack directly the myths which often rob them of influence over the public, the government, and often over trade union members themselves. To attack the myth of big labor, unions must do more outreach in local communities. They must convince the public that trade unions are not narrowly conceived interest groups, but rather associations dedicated to improving community life, with a special concern for those who are powerless as individuals. This requires a broadening of the conception of labor unions, the scope of labor union activities, and of citizen access to labor union decision making. Labor unions or groups sponsored by them should be active on every issue of local political importance. At the same time, interested members of the community should be encouraged to attend union meetings and participate in union activities. In doing so, unions can build community support for their positions on labor issues as well as educate the public and their own members on the important links between community life and the workplace.[83]

Attacking the myths and building community support for labor union activities require the use of the media and educational facilities. The labor movement must directly and explicitly counter the idea that management is the locus of entrepreneurial skill and technical expertise and the notion that a hierarchical command structure is the most efficient form of managing economic activities. A "What are bosses for?" campaign should be begun on radio, TV, newspapers, and in schools to show that workers can regulate their own activities and that much of the role of professional managers is to make sure that workers do not do so.

In general, workers and unions need better access to the news, entertainment, and advertising media as well as the educational system. The labor movement needs a national daily newspaper of general circulation. It needs radio and TV stations in major metropolitan areas. It needs thoughtful and clever dramatic and comic renderings of the lives of workers and the role of the labor movement in those lives presented regularly on prime-time, network television. Without these, its message will always be at the mercy of productions, publications, and stations which are in themselves business interests and which cater to business interests. Labor history and the progressive and innovative role of labor unions and workers must be centerpieces of elementary and secondary school curriculums in history, social studies, economics, government and civics.

The labor movement must strenuously and explicitly take up demands for the regulation of business enterprises in the interest of workers and communities. Stability of worklife is more important to most workers than mobility of capital. In doing so, labor must form solid links with other groups seeking to limit the power of business interests over community life and government. These include civil rights activists, environmentalists, feminists, consumer groups, antinuclear groups, and groups opposed to U.S. foreign and military policies. These links are not simply logrolling and accommodation. The position of each of these groups represents a partial challenge to the precedence of the interests of capital over the lives of people. The labor movement, at least in its original conception, represents the largest and most encompassing version of this same challenge. Therefore, these linkages are not merely of convenience, but are logical and appropriate for establishing a progressive movement that places people before capital. Furthermore, this purpose should not preclude the use of labor's capital (in the form of pension funds) to make economically prudent, but politically conscious, investments.

The recommendation to develop political unionism envisions active efforts to establish a left-wing political party as an encouragement to the nonlabor left and as an educational forum for the full and public discussion of major alternatives to existing policies. The formation of such a party, even without great electoral strength, would at least discourage the Democratic party from moving rightward and dumping the concerns of the labor movement along with those of blacks, feminists, and the poor.

In the following chapters, we will see how these recommendations hold up in light of the comparison with the French cases. Because French workers have developed a more political unionism and (in the case of steel plant closings) have been considerably more militant, this comparison will help support, refute, or alter the recommendations for a more militant and political unionism in the United States.

Appendix: Recommendations of the Labor Union Study Tour

1. Federal fiscal and monetary policies should be implemented to fulfill the letter and spirit of the Full Employment Act of 1946 and the Humphrey–Hawkins Full Employment and Balanced Growth Act of 1978.
2. Advanced notice of impending layoffs, dismissals and plant shutdowns should be given to government, affected trade unions and individual workers as soon as the employer contemplates the decision. Since in many cases in the United States the lag time between shutdown and a new startup or conversion of an abandoned facility is three to five years, and in many other cases conversion is never made, then a one-year mandatory prenotification period is not unreasonable.

3. Employers owe a duty to show cause why they must shut down, move operations, reduce the work force or make other planned dismissals. Accurate information about a firm's financial condition, costs and profits are essential to evaluate the necessity of a recision (sic), move or shutdown. Production of these data and financial records must be subject to subpoena powers, and not left to voluntary compliance or to time-consuming legal discovery proceedings. It should be mandatory for companies to bargain with unions over shutdown and cutback decisions, not just over the effects of those decisions as at the present time. The company must offer to begin such bargaining well in advance of implementing its decision.

4. Reasonable proposals by trade unions, impacted workers, and government to avert shutdown or dismissals must be given a fair hearing and guaranteed a fair chance to be implemented.

5. Economic and social studies assessing employment, income, housing market and general business activity within the impacted community—made by a proper government agency—are mandatory.

6. Failure to comply with the advance notice, duty to provide accurate information, mandatory impact study and other requirements should invoke stiff monetary penalties. In the event a firm proceeds to move or shut down or implement a recision (sic) after failure to show cause, it should lose federal tax incentives, credits and subsidies, be liable for the full cost of adjustment assistance and in certain circumstances face debarment from bidding on federal contracts.

7. Unless show-cause hearings determine otherwise, development of an alternative production plan for an abandoned facility is also mandatory and must include a survey of market potential for alternative products or services. Alternative production plans which are developed should meet emerging or unmet national priorities.

8. Targeted federal procurement should be utilized in support of alternative production plans, and to prevent dislocation.

9. Adjustment assistance for displaced workers, including severance pay, mandatory transfer rights (with no reduction in benefits or pay), guaranteed social security credits, health benefits and adequate income maintenance benefits

are to be provided by the company until the individual is re-employed. Adequate retraining, mobility assistance and guaranteed employer-paid relocation expenses must be provided, as well as improved voluntary early retirement benefits.

10. In cases of bankruptcy, receivership or going out of business, costs of impact statements, adjustment assistance and alternative production plans are to be borne by the federal government.

11. There should be temporary short workweek programs which could be implemented when job and income loss can be averted by this means. Benefits could be financed through the unemployment compensation system, as in Western Europe.

12. Strict curbs on overtime and hiring and dismissal freezes shall be imposed on companies during the mandatory period of advance notice.

13. Under certain circumstances, and with careful safeguards against abuse, corporations and communities should be provided temporary federal subsidies to insure continuity of employment, while alternative production plans and job creation programs are being made. Public works projects should be coordinated into the conversion program.

14. Firms should be required to set aside a portion of their profits in a tax-free Investment Reserve Fund, to be used at the direction of the proper government agency for investment purposes only in a community or region marked by high unemployment and a declining economy, targeted to provide jobs for prospective or past victims of economic dislocation. Large corporations should be required to disclose detailed plant-by-plant investment plans to an appropriate agency of the federal government. These plans should extend several years into the future, and be updated on a regular basis.

15. Tax incentives such as Investment Tax Credit, accelerated depreciation and start-up credits should be permitted only if a firm remains, expands, or makes new investment in the community or region, without causing dislocation.

16. Credit should be allocated, through special low interest rates, to those firms investing in new plant and equipment to offset economic dislocation and meet designated national priorities.

17. The nation's Employment Services must be upgraded and coordinated with mandatory listing of job vacancies, other than those to be filled by transfer or promotion, required from employers. During the one-year period of notice, workers should have paid time off to look for a new job.
18. Communities that lose tax revenues as a result of a plant shutdown must be compensated in order that vital services are not impaired or interrupted.
19. State and local tax abatements and tax exempt industrial development revenue bonds used to lure plants and industries from one region, state or community to another must be abolished.
20. When federal programs and actions such as energy policies, environmental standards, international trade policy and military and civilian procurement decisions result in economic dislocation, then the federal government has a special obligation to implement job creation and adjustment assistance programs to mitigate the impact and facilitate the maintenance of a strong and viable local economy. The level and duration of benefits should be at least comparable to those provided under the Amtrak, Conrail and Redwood programs.
21. Unemployment insurance and Workers' Compensation laws must be federalized, with uniform benefit levels and qualification standards throughout the 50 states.
22. To insure uniform labor policy among the states and to prevent unfair competition based on national labor laws, Section 14(b) of the National Labor Relations Act must be repealed and comprehensive labor law reform enacted. To prevent victimization of their members by runaway employers, unions should be granted automatic recognition, with contracts continuing in full force and effect, at newly opened or acquired runaway plants. Rights of successorship must also be guaranteed, to help protect workers in plant shutdown situations.
23. Bankruptcy laws must be revised to protect workers and guarantee satisfaction of their claims, including pay in lieu of mandatory notice and maintenance of health, pension and other benefits.
24. Federal anti-trust laws must be strengthened with respect to corporate mergers and acquisitions and must be designed to apply to conglomerate mergers, which may not

have anti-competitive consequences, but do result in economic dislocation and undue concentration of economic,
political and social power. "Efficiency" should not be the
sole test used to justify conglomerate mergers; protection
against economic dislocations is a valid criterion as well.

25. Foreign investment by U.S.-based corporations must be
licensed so as to meet acceptable wage, benefit, hours,
retirement, safety and health and environmental protection
standards. Such licenses should be granted only upon assurance that job loss and other economic dislocation in the U.S.
will not ensue.

26. The Department of Labor must gather, collect, and period-
ically report on a regular basis plant closing, plant moving,
and other economic dislocation data on a state-by-state
basis.

27. To coordinate implementation of the above recommendations, appropriate labor market bodies at the national,
regional, and community levels—as well as workplace adjustment and planning groups when needed—must be
created.

Endnotes

1. Kenneth Noble, "U.S. Study Details Employment Shift," *New York Times*,
June 8, 1985, pp. 1, 28, reporting the results of a Dept. of Labor study
commissioned by Congress and released on June 7, 1985.

2. Barry Bluestone and Bennett Harrison, *The Deindustrialization of America*
(New York: Basic Books, 1982), pp. 27–40. Bluestone and Harrison and this
author base their estimates of job generation and destruction on the analysis
of David Birch, *The Job Generation Process* (Cambridge, Mass.: MIT
Program on Neighborhood & Regional Change, 1979). While a Brookings
Institute study has challenged some of the Birch findings, Birch's response to
the Brookings study seems convincing, see Catherine Armington and Mar-
garet Odle, "Small Business—How Many Jobs," *Brookings Review* (Winter
1982), pp. 14–17 and David Birch and Susan McCracken, *The Small Business
Share of Job Creation: Lessons Learned from the Use of a Longitudinal File*
(Cambridge, Mass.: MIT Program on Neighborhood & Regional Change,
1982); cf. Candee Harris, *The Magnitude of Job Loss from Plant Closings
and the Generation of Replacement Jobs: Some Recent Evidence* (Washington, D.C.: Brookings Institute, 1983); for more recent discouraged worker
statistics and analysis of the recovery, see *Employment in America: Illusory
Recovery in a Decade of Decline* (Washington: D.C.: Full Employment
Action Council, 1985).

3. Emma Rothschild, "Reagan and the Real America," *New York Review of Books,* Feb. 5, 1981, pp. 12–18; Birch, note 2; U.S. Dept. of Labor, Bureau of Labor Statistics, *Handbook of Labor Statistics* (Washington, D.C.: U.S. Government Printing Office, 1983).

4. Bluestone and Harrison, note 2, pp. 27–30.

5. See, e.g., Terry Buss and F. Stevens Redburn, *Shutdown at Youngstown* (Albany, N.Y.: SUNY Press, 1983); Susan Cunningham, "Shock of Layoff Felt Deep Inside Family Circle," *The Christian Science Monitor,* Jan. 8, 1983; "Statement of Max Mont" in House Subcommittees on Employment Opportunities and Labor–Management Relations of Committee on Education and Labor, *Joint Hearing on Plant Closing, H.R. 2847* (Washington, D.C.: USGPO, 1983); cf. *Employment in America,* note 2.

6. Bluestone and Harrison, note 2, pp. 49–107 and notes accompanying text; John Raines, Lenora Berson, and David Gracie (eds.), *Community and Capital in Conflict: Plant Closings and Job Losses* (Philadelphia: Temple Univ. Press, 1982); House Subcommittee on Labor–Management Relations of the Committee on Education and Labor, *Worker Dislocation, Capital Flight, and Plant Closings, H.R. 2847* (Washington, D.C.: USGPO, 1984); U.S. Senate Committee on Labor and Human Resources, *Hearings on the Employee Protection and Community Stabilization Act of 1979* (Washington: USGPO, 1980); cf. items cited in note 16, below. For an analysis of plant closing research and recommendations for future projects, see Donald Kennedy (ed.), *Labor and Reindustrialization* (University Park: Pennsylvania State Dept. of Labor Studies, 1984) and J. Gordus, P. Jarley, and L. Ferman, *Plant Closings and Economic Dislocation* (Kalamazoo, Kan.: W.E. Upjohn Institute, 1981). For British plant closing research, see Doreen Massey and Richard Meegan, *The Anatomy of Job Loss* (London: Methuen, 1982). French research will be noted in the next chapter.

7. *First National Maintenance Corp. v. NLRB,* 452 U.S. 666, 680–82 (1981).

8. Dept. of Labor, Bureau of Labor Statistics, *Major Collective Bargaining Agreements: Plant Movement, Interplant Transfer, and Relocation Allowances* (Washington, D.C.: U.S. Dept. of Labor, 1981); *Collective Bargaining, Negotiations and Contracts* vol. 2, (Washington, D.C.: Bureau of National Affairs, 1983; Bob Baugh, "Shutdown: Mill Closures and Woodworkers," undated memo for Dept. of Research, Education and Collective Bargaining of the International Woodworkers of America.

9. *First National Maintenance Corp. v. NLRB,* note 7; cf. *National Labor Relations Board v. Bildisco & Bildisco,* 104 S.Ct. 1188 (1984); *Milwaukee Spring Division of Illinois Coil Spring,* 115 LRRM 1065 (1984) and *Otis Elevator,* 115 LRRM 1281 (1984).

10. *Handbook of Labor Statistics* (Washington, D.C.: USGPO, 1981), pp. 169, 400–14; cf. Henry S. Farber, "The Extent of Unionization in the United States," in Thomas A. Kochan (ed.), *Challenges and Choices for American Labor* (Cambridge, Mass.: MIT Press, 1985).

11. Everett M. Kassalow, "The Crisis in the World Steel Industry: Union–Management Responses in Four Countries," in *Proceedings of the 37th Annual Meeting of the Industrial Relations Research Association* (Madison, Wisc.: IRRA, 1984), pp. 341–51.

12. Staughton Lynd, "Investment Decisions and the Quid Pro Quo Myth," *Case Western Reserve Law Review* 29 (1979), pp. 396–428; Sharon Simon, "Plant Closings and the Law of Collective Bargaining," in Donald Kennedy (ed.), *Labor and Reindustrialization*, note 6, pp. 69–93; Patricia A. Greenfield, "Plant Closing Obligations Under the National Labor Relations Act," in Antone Aboud (ed.), *Plant Closing Legislation* (Ithaca, N.Y.: Industrial & Labor Relations Press, 1984), pp. 13–32. Recently, workers have begun lawsuits to challenge closings where employers, at least verbally, had assured job security.

13. National Commission on Unemployment Compensation, *Unemployment Compensation: Studies and Research*, 3 vols. (Washington, D.C.: USGPO, 1980); D. Runner, "Unemployment Insurance: Changes Enacted During 1981," *Monthly Labor Review* 105, no. 2 (Feb. 1982), pp. 16–23; *Social Security Bulletin* 44, no. 9 (Sept. 1981), p. 50.

14. Michael Podgursky, "Labor Market Policy and Structural Adjustment," in U.S. Congress, Joint Economic Committee (ed.), *Policies for Industrial Growth in a Competitive World: A Volume of Essays* (Washington, D.C.: USGPO, 1984), pp. 71–96; John Corson et al. *Final Report: Survey of Trade Adjustment Recipients* (Princeton: N.J.: Mathematica Policy Research, 1979); cf. "The Reagan Budget: The Figures," *New York Times*, Feb. 20, 1981, pp. 1, 17.

15. "Lost Medical Care for Jobless: Cost May Be Health or Lives," *New York Times*, Mar. 7, 1983, pp. A1, B9.

16. Charles Craypo and William Davisson, "Plant Shutdown, Collective Bargaining, and Job and Employment Experience of Displaced Brewery Workers," *Labor Studies Journal* 7 (Winter 1983), pp. 195–215; Bluestone and Harrison, note 2, pp. 49–81; Harry Gilman, *Advance Notice of Plant Closures* (Washington, D.C.: U.S. Dept. of Labor, 1977); David Smith and Patrick McGuigan, *"Youngstown Is Not Unique . . .": The Public Policy Implications of Plant Closings and Runaways* (Technical Development Corp.: Washington, D.C.: 1978); Arlene Holen, *Losses to Workers Displaced by Plant Closure or Layoff* (Washington, D.C.: Public Research Institute, 1976); Louis Jacobson, *Earnings Losses of Workers Displaced from Manufacturing Industries* (Washington, D.C.: Public Research Institute, 1976); cf. works cited in note 6.

17. Labor Union Study Tour, *Economic Dislocation* (UAW, USWA, IAM, 1979).

18. Ibid., p. 2.

19. Ibid., p. 3.

20. *H.R. 5040, S. 1608*, 96th Cong., 1st sess. (1979).

21. National Employment Priorities Act of 1974, *H.R. 13541*, 93d Cong., 2d sess. (1974); see Technical Development Corp. study, note 16, pp. 16–18.

22. *Maine Revised Statutes*, tit. 26, sec. 625–B (1971); See generally Nancy Folbre, Julia Leighton, and Melissa Roderick, "Plant Closings and Their Regulation in Maine, 1971–82," *Industrial and Labor Relations Review* 37 (Jan. 1984), pp. 185–96. For evidence indicating that some controls on plant closings, particularly with regard to absentee controlled or conglomerate firms, have little negative and some positive effect on local investment, see Charles Craypo, "The Deindustrialization of a Factory Town: Plant Closings and Phasedowns in South Bend, Indiana, 1954–83," in Kennedy (ed.), *Labor*

and Reindustrialization, note 6, pp. 27–67; cf. Birch, note 2; Birch and McCracken, note 2; David L. Barkley, "Plant Ownership Characteristics and the Locational Stability of Rural Iowa Manufacturers," *Land Economics* 54 (Feb. 1978); Robert Anderson and David Barkley, "Rural Manufacturers' Characteristics and Probability of Plant Closings," *Growth and Change* 13 (Jan. 1982), pp. 2–8; Robert Stern and Howard Aldrich, *The Effect of Absentee Firm Control on Local Community Welfare: A Survey* (Ithaca, N.Y.: New York State School of Industrial & Labor Relations, 1979); Michael Booth, *Ownership of Industry* (Cambridge, Mass.: Center for Community Economic Development, 1972); John Udell, *Social and Economic Consequences of the Merger Movement in Wisconsin* (Madison: Wisconsin Economic Services, 1969). For an international perspective, see D. Van Den Bulcke, J. J. Boddewyn, B. Martens and P. Klemmer, *Politiques d'Investissement, Réductions ou Cessations d'Activités de Multinationales en Europe* (Paris: Presses Universitaire de France–Communauté Economique Européen Imprimerie, 1979), pp. 16–22. With regard to the effects of conglomerates on local businesses and communities, see Attorney General of the United States, *Conglomerate Mergers, Small Business, and the Scope of Existing Anti-Merger Statutes* (Washington, D.C.: Dept. of Justice, 1979), p. 14. See generally Subcommittee on Antitrust and Restraint of Trade Activities Effecting Small Business of the House Committee on Small Business, *Hearings on Conglomerate Mergers—Their Effects on Small Business and Local Communities* (Washington, D.C.: USGPO, 1980); cf. Julien Savary, *Les Multinationales Françaises* (Paris: Presses Universitaires de France, 1981).

23. Iver Peterson, "Company Towns Without Companies Lack Remedies," *New York Times*, Feb. 3, 1981, p. 23.

24. Everett M. Kassalow, "Collective Bargaining in the Grip of Structural Change," paper delivered at the 33rd Annual Convention of the Industrial Relations Research Association, Denver, 1980.

25. Staughton Lynd, *The Fight Against Shutdowns* (San Pedro, Calif.: Singlejack Books, 1982), pp. 50–53.

26. Technical Development Corp., note 16, pp. 17–18; Barry Bluestone and Bennett Harrison, *Capital and Communities* (Washington, D.C.: Progressive Alliance, 1980), pp. 256–57.

27. *Wisconsin Statutes Annotated*, sec. 109.07 (1975); cf. Iver Peterson, note 23; Antone Aboud and Sanford Schram, "An Overview of Plant Closing Legislation and Issues," in Aboud (ed.), *Plant Closing Legislation*, note 12, p. 34.

28. Bennett Harrison, "Comparing European and American Experience with Plant Closing Laws," in *36th Annual Proceedings of the Industrial Relations Research Association* (Madison, Wisc.: IRRA, 1984), p. 125.

29. Bluestone and Harrison, *Deindustrialization of America*, note 2, p. 238; Ed Kelly, "Plant Closings Legislation: The Ohio Experience," in W. Schweke (ed.), *Plant Closings Strategy Packet* (Washington, D.C.: Conference on Alternative State & Local Government Policies, 1980); speech and interview with Ira Arlook at Runaway Shops Conference, Lincoln, R.I., March 29, 1980.

30. Technical Development Corp., note 16, pp. 12–14.

31. *H.R. 11222*, 95th Cong., 2d sess. (1978).

32. Winston Williams, "Ohio: The Beat of the Industrial Heartland," *New York Times*, Oct. 12, 1980, pp. Fl, F22–23; Bluestone and Harrison, *Deindustrialization of America*, note 2, pp. 35–40, 69–72.
33. Schweke, note 29, pp. 1–2.
34. *S. 1609*, 9th Cong., 1st sess.; (1979); *S. 2400*, 96th Cong., 2d sess. (1980).
35. Portions of the Voluntary Job Preservation and Community Stabilization Act were incorporated into *S. 388* and *S. 918*, 96th Cong., 2d sess. (1980).
36. Senate Committee on Labor and Human Resources, *Hearing on S.1609 Oct. 29, 1979* (Washington, D.C.: USGPO, 1980).
37. Daniel D. Cook, "Laws to Curb Plant Closings," *Industry Week*, Feb. 4, 1980, p. 41.
38. *H.R. 7315*, 96th Cong., 2d sess.; *H.R. 565*, 97th Cong., 1st sess.; Richard Nelson, "State Labor Legislation Enacted in 1981," *Monthly Labor Review* 105 (Jan. 1982), p. 29; see generally, Note, "Advance Notice of Plant Closings: Toward National Legislation," *Journal of Law Reform* 14, no. 2 (Winter 1981), pp. 283–319; Aboud and Schram, note 27.
39. Aboud and Schram, note 27, p. 42.
40. In Rhode Island, as will be more fully discussed below, Rep. Zygmunt Friedemann has proposed *H. 5843*, the Business and Community Preservation Act, and Reps. Cardente, Vanner and Sherman have proposed *H. 5113*, an amendment to the Rhode Island Industrial Facilities Corporation Act. In Massachusetts, two new state agencies have been proposed to deal with the reinvestment aspects of closing and closed plants. These are the Massachusetts Industrial Revitalization Corporation and the Division of Industrial Facilities Viability. Cf. "Coalition to Save Jobs Update," *CLOC Newsletter* 4, no. 1, (Spring 1983), p. 4. Michigan has recently adopted Public Act 44, which requires that 60 days' notification of a closing be given to the Michigan Dept. of Labor in cases where an employee buyout could be facilitated by the department's assistance, Gordus, Jarley, and Ferman, note 6, p. 60; Harrison, note 28, pp. 125–26; Tamar Lewin, "Workers' Rights in a Closing Tested," *New York Times*, July 19, 1984, pp. D1, D23.
41. The statistics are from the Rhode Island Dept. of Employment Security, the Rhode Island Dept. of Economic Development, and the Federal Reserve Bank of Boston, *New England Economic Indicators* (1983–1985).
42. As a member of the Coalition to Save Jobs and the Community Labor Organizing Committee, I was active in the campaign to secure the adoption of plant closing legislation. I was part of the subcommittee that redrafted the comprehensive bill in 1980. Much of this information comes from formal and informal interviews with the participants in the events described as well as from the local press. The 1979 bill in the Rhode Island House of Representatives was *H. 5264*, the Employee and Community Assistance Act.
43. Rhode Island, State Senate, *S. 2248*, the Severance Pay Liability Act. (1980).
44. Rhode Island, House of Representatives, *H. 7796*, the Business Closings and Factory Relocation Act (1980).
45. Statement of Silvio Santilli at the Runaway Shops Conference, Lincoln, R.I., Mar. 29, 1980.
46. Statement of Winnie Carvalho at Runaway Shops Conference, Ibid.
47. Quoted in *CLOC Newsletter* (Apr. 1980), p. 4. The workers' compensation

issue involved the acceptance and attempts at ameliorating the effects of a business proposal to limit compensation payments. This legislation was finally passed without much labor input.

48. The foregoing information was taken from the minutes of the meetings of Community Labor Organizing Committee and from interviews with several participants in the Providence and State Labor Councils' meetings during the period of Aug. 7, 1980 to Feb. 12, 1981.

49. Rhode Island, House of Representatives, *H. 5400*, an Act Relating to Extended Medical Benefits (1981).

50. Rhode Island, House of Representatives, *H. 6266*, the Employee Readjustment Act (1981).

51. John Kiffney, "Laid-Off Workers Shouldn't Lose Health Insurance, Panel Is Told," *Providence Journal* Mar. 20, 1981, p. A14.

52. Ibid.

53. "Letters to the Editor," *Providence Journal*, May 7, 1981, p. A20. Of course, no such legislation existed in Rhode Island at any time. Studies done in the states where some plant closing legislation has existed indicate that it does not cause the exodus of business; see research cited in note 22, above.

54. "R.I. Legislature's Pro-Labor Image Begins to Change," *Providence Journal*, Apr. 26, 1981, p. D5.

55. Rhode Island, House of Representatives, *H. 7703*, an Act Relating to Rights of Employees in Plant Closings (1982).

56. Rhode Island, House of Representatives, *H. 7703 Substitute A*, Joint Resolution Creating a Special Legislative Commission to Study the Problems Caused by the Closing of Industrial Plants in the State of Rhode Island (1982).

57. Rhode Island Strategic Development Commission, *The Greenhouse Compact*, 2 vols. (Providence, R.I.: Strategic Development Commission, 1984), Pt. IV "Improving Rhode Island's Economy"; Letter from the Coalition to Save Jobs (CLOC) to supporters of plant closing legislation, Jan. 5, 1983; *CLOC Newsletter*, Feb. 1982, pp. 1–2; cf. William Hudson, Mark Hyde, and John Carroll, "Corporatist Policymaking and State Economic Development," paper delivered at the Workshop on Public Policy, University of Guelph, Guelph, Ontario, May 1985, p. 6; Joseph Goodrich, "R.I. Business Climate Gauged," *Providence Journal*, July 9, 1985, pp. B1, B2.

58. *The Greenhouse Compact*, note 57, vol. 2, pp. 272–40, 776–826; but see, Joseph Goodrich, "A Fundamental Shift Gives State a Business Look," *Providence Sunday Journal*, June 30, 1985, p. F3. For research indicating what does influence business location and investment decisions, see Roger Schmenner, "Choosing New Industrial Capacity: On-Site Expansion, Branching, and Relocation," *Quarterly Journal of Economics* 59 (Aug. 1980), pp. 103–19; Roger Schmenner, *The Manufacturing Location Decision*, report to the Economic Development Administration, March 1978; cf. A Touraine, V. Ahtik, S. Ostrowetsky-Zygel and M. Castells, "Mobilité des entreprises et structures urbaines," *Sociologie du Travail* 9, no. 4 (1967), pp. 369–405; M. Appert and R. Maguet, *Les effêts sur l'emploi de la politique de décentralisation dans le departement de la Seine-Saint-Denis* (Paris: Ministère de Travail, 1971), pp. 14–18. While the internal negotiations of the

commission were subject to some secrecy, they are now being discussed more openly. This information comes from informal discussions with commission staff and the statement of Ira Magaziner at several meetings.

59. Testimony of William Delevan at the "Hearing on Plant Closings" of the New York State Senate, N.Y., Dec. 7, 1979.
60. Senate Committee on Labor and Human Resources, *Hearing on the Employee Protection and Community Stabilization Act of 1979* (Washington, D.C.: USGPO, 1980), pp. 168–69.
61. Richard Madden, "Connecticut Moves to Aid Workers," *New York Times*, June 5, 1983, p. 59.
62. Peter Capelli, "Union Gains Under Concession Bargaining," in Proceedings of the IRRA 36th Annual Meeting, note 28, p. 35.
63. Gerald Glyde, "Managing Economic Change: Labor's Role," in Kennedy (ed.), *Labor and Reindustrialization*, note 6, pp. 1–26; Anthony Mazzocchi, "Changing Economic Realities and the Changing Role of Unions," *New York University Review of Law and Social Change* 11, no. 1 (1982–1983), pp. 8–10; Howard Lesnick, "The Structure of Post-War Labor Relations," ibid., pp. 142–43. The 1983–84 version of the National Employment Priorities Act, *H.R. 2847*, 98th Cong., 1st sess. was easily bottled in committee. Reps. William Clay, William Ford and Silvio Conte expect a similar fate for their version, *H.R. 1616*, 99th Cong., 1st sess. The state efforts are meeting with no more success, "Plant Closing Laws Run into Opposition in Some States," *Wall Street Journal*, Mar. 26, 1985, p. 1.
64. Quoted in James B. Atleson, *Values and Assumptions in American Labor Law* (Amherst: Univ. of Massachusetts Press, 1983), p. 148. Wilson's concern at the time was the UAW's radical demand that GM bargain over pensions; however, behind that demand was a demand that GM open its financial books to the union to prove its inability to grant increased benefits and wages.
65. "Democrats and Labor Need Each Other, R.I. Unionist Says," *Providence Evening Bulletin*, July 17, 1984, p. A5; Peter Gosselin, "Labor, Business Arrive at Crossroad," *Providence Journal*, Sept. 12, 1982, pp. A1, A10.
66. The analysis in this section owes much to Harry Braverman, *Labor and Monopoly Capital: The Degradation of Work in the Twentieth Century* (New York: Monthly Review Press, 1974); Manuel Castells, *The Urban Question* (Cambridge, Mass.: MIT Press, 1980); "Introduction" and Sumner Rosen, "The United States: The American Industrial Relations System in Jeopardy," in Solomon Barkin (ed.), *Worker Militancy and its Consequences* (New York: Praeger, 1983); Stanley Aronowitz, *False Promises* (New York: Random House, 1973); and Staughton Lynd, "Investment Decisions and the *Quid Pro Quo* Myth," note 12; see generally, "Colloquium: Labor at the Crossroads," *New York University Review of Law and Social Change* 11, no. 1 (1982–1983).
67. Karl Klare, "Judicial Deradicalization of the Wagner Act and the Origins of Modern Legal Consciousness, 1937–1941," *Minnesota Law Review* 62 (1978), pp. 265–339; Mazzocchi, note 63, pp. 7–10.
68. *NLRB v. Mackay Radio and Telegraph Co.*, 304 U.S. 333 (1938) in which the Court held that Section 13 of the NLRA barring construction of the Act "so as to interfere with or impede or diminish in any way the right to strike" did not preclude an employer from hiring workers to replace strikers and to

refuse to rehire strikers whose places were taken by newly hired workers. This interpretation drastically undercut the Act's protection of the right to strike.

69. Atleson, note 64, pp. 19–34.

70. 398 U.S. 235 (1970); cf. Kark Klare, "Critical Theory and Labor Relations Law," in David Kairys, *The Politics of Law* (New York: Pantheon, 1982), pp. 67–72.

71. The fragility of these successes has become evident since 1982 with the reduction of TRA benefits to UI levels, the dismantling of the enforcement mechanisms of OSHA, and the encouragement of businesses to opt out of pension programs altogether by promoting the Individual Retirement Account and Keogh plans.

72. Sumner Rosen, "Changing Economic Realities and the Changing Economic Role of Unions," *New York University Review of Law and Social Change*, 11 (1982–1983), pp. 18–19; cf. William Gould, *A Primer on Labor Law* (Cambridge, Mass.: MIT Press, 1982).

73. National Labor Relations Board, *NLRB Report* (Washington, D.C.: USGPO, 1979), p. 21; William Serrin, "Union Membership Falls Sharply; Decline Expected to Be Permanent," *New York Times*, May 31, 1983, pp. A1, A16.

74. "'84 Labor Contracts Reported Producing 3% Increases in Pay," *New York Times*, Apr. 29, 1984, p. 55; Bureau of Labor Statistics, *Handbook of Labor Statistics* (Washington, D.C.: USGPO, 1980, 1983); cf. Samuel Bowles, David Gordon, and Thomas Weisskopf, *Beyond the Wasteland* (Garden City, N.J.: Doubleday, 1984), pp. 19–33.

75. John L. Oshinski, "The Challenges of Organizing," *New York University Review of Law and Social Change* 11, no. 1 (1982–1983), pp. 57–66; Mazzochi, note 63, p. 25.

76. Oshinski, note 75, p. 79.

77. Interview with Peter Gosselin in *CLOC Newsletter*, Jan. 1982, pp. 1, 3. The Providence Journal Co. publishes the only two major daily newspapers in Rhode Island. Machinists at Brown & Sharpe, a R.I. based tool manufacturer, have been on strike for well over two years in the longest American strike on record. No end other than the drifting away of the strikers seems to be in sight at this time.

78. AFL-CIO Committee on the Evolution of Work, *The Changing Situation of Workers and Their Unions* (Washington, D.C.: AFL-CIO, 1985), pp. 13.

79. Hudson, et al., note 57, pp. 17–18.

80. Kenneth Noble, "In 50 Years Unions Move from Foes to Fans of Labor Board," *New York Times*, July 9, 1985, p. A14.

81. Daniel Bell, "The Subversion of Collective Bargaining," in Gerry Hunnius, David Garson, and John Case, *Workers' Control* (New York: Random House, 1973), pp. 120–36. For further evidence of "price administration," even during economic crisis, see Leslie Wayne, "Business Struggles to Raise Its Prices," *New York Times*, Mar. 6, 1983, pp. F1, F31.

82. It will be noted that many of these recommendations have been made in the past by long-time friends of the labor movement as well as by the AFL-CIO Committee on the Evolution of Work.

83. The Youngstown–Longwy comparison in Chapter 4 will point up the effects of a great difference in community support for and solidarity with those fighting plant closings.

Chapter 3

PLANT CLOSINGS AND LAYOFF REGULATION IN FRANCE: THE MYTHS UNDER FIRE

In this chapter, we shall identify the role of the myths of big labor, the business climate, and legality in France's legal and administrative scheme for regulating plant closings and layoffs. It should not be surprising that the form and role of these myths is different than in the United States. An initial difference is in France's labor–management relations system. Several unions may, and often do, represent people from the same job category in the same plant. A union need not represent a majority of the plant's workers to be recognized for collective bargaining or as the representative of workers for any other lawful purpose. Secondly, the French government plays an important role in extending benefits negotiated by one or more unions to other workers who were not represented in the initial negotiations. Thirdly, unlike the United States, France has a comprehensive scheme for regulating closings and economic layoffs.

Myth and Power in a New Context

Despite these differences, it is important to recall the content of the myths as they appeared in U.S. politics. The myth of big labor promoted an image of organized labor as excessively powerful both in politics and in labor–management relations. This excessive power was held to add unnecessary costs to and restrictions on business activities, thereby reducing the ability of business to compete with nonunion or foreign enterprises. Union power was said to be maintained by corrupt and/or authoritarian leadership whose interests did not necessarily correspond with the interests of rank and file workers.

The closely related myth of the business climate promoted the view that any move by government or unions to aid workers or to strengthen the labor movement was a burden on business interests and reduced the attractiveness of investment in the businesses or the jurisdiction affected. Implicit in both these myths is the notion that business interests, rather than trade union interests, more closely reflect the public interest, including the interests of workers.

The myth of legality supposed legal and administrative procedures that were evenhanded in protecting worker and business interests and that gave each side a full, fair, and expeditious hearing and resolution of a dispute. Workers could have confidence that the purpose of the legal and administrative procedures was to achieve justice and that the view of justice that the procedures embodied reflected the workers' view of justice.

As we saw in Chapter 2, these myths are poorly supported and often contradicted by the evidence. Nevertheless, they have had a strong impact on the perceptions of the public, government officials, and even workers themselves. They operate to the detriment of the interests of workers. The myths constitute part of the second and third faces of power (the hidden faces), in that they operate to restrict and stifle the full public debate of the issues and the gathering and consideration of the evidence. We shall see if these or similar myths achieve the same impact in France.

The Economics of Plant Closings and Workers' Interests

The Changing Employment Structure

Like the United States, France is undergoing a major employment shift characterized by the growth of the office, service, and commercial sectors of the economy and a decline in industrial employment. Between 1974 and 1981, the number of jobs in the manufacture of consumer goods decreased by 261,000, in the manufacture of equipment by 182,000, in the manufacture of production materials by 251,000, and in the construction industry by 194,000. The recession of 1974–75 was a clear watershed in this trend. From 1969 to 1974, these industries increased their employment by 570,000, while from 1975 to 1981 their employment decreased by 903,000. From 1969 to 1978, the commercial sector had a net employment increase of 200,000 jobs per year. This increase slowed greatly to a total of 100,000 jobs between 1979 and 1981. The shifts in employment caused by these opposing movements pushed the tertiary sector's share of total employment from 51.9% in 1974 to 57% in 1980 and have reduced industry's share of employment from 37.8% in 1974 to 34.2% in 1980. The most recent census figures confirm that this trend is continuing, but at a slower rate.[1]

Since the 1974 watershed, the creation of jobs has occurred primarily in firms of fewer than 50 employees. These firms accounted for 46.9% of all employees in 1981, as opposed to 42.8% in 1975. By contrast, firms of 200 or more employees accounted for 31.2% of all jobs in 1981, down from 35.7% in 1975. The reduction of employment in industry has hit skilled workers especially hard. Their representation on the unemployment rolls has gone from 37.3% of the unemployed in 1973 to 54.1% in 1981. Employment has become more precarious. The number of "temporary" employees —until recently unprotected by layoff regulations—has doubled since 1977, and the number of protected "permanent" employees laid off for economic reasons has increased by 50%.[2]

There have been important regional consequences of the changing employment structure.[3] Between 1975 and 1980, the Mediterranean and Atlantic Coast regions have experienced an increase in jobs at the same time that their unemployment rates have been the highest in the country. The Parisian region and the Rhône–Alpes region (in which Lyon and Valence are situated) have had relatively low unemployment rates but only a slight increase in jobs. In the Lorraine region, where massive job destruction has occurred, the unemployment rate has remained relatively low.

These differences are explained by the influx of workers, including immigrants, to the most industrially dynamic regions such as Provence–Alpes–Côte d'Azur (in which are situated Marseille, Arles, Nîmes, Fos, and Nice), the reduced attraction of previously dynamic regions such as Paris (Ile-de-France) and Lyon (Rhône-Alpes), and the massive exodus of workers from the

severely depressed regions such as the Lorraine. Only in the older
industrial regions of the North and Northwest (Nord–Pas-de-
Calais, Haute–Normandie, and Basse–Normandie) has the decrease in jobs been fully reflected in high unemployment rates.

The import of these statistics in France, as in the United States,
is that they reflect a change of the employment structure toward
jobs that are less well paid, less skilled, less likely to be unionized,
more likely to be part-time or temporary, where working conditions are more oppressive and less likely to be regulated, and in
parts of the country other than where job destruction has been
most severe. Unemployment has been even more severe since
1982 due to the deceleration of job creation in the tertiary sector
that resulted from the policy of austerity imposed by the Socialist
government.[4] Recent statistics also indicate a longstanding and a
continuing interest of workers in plant closing and layoff regulation to further the security of their employment.

The Magnitude and Impact of Economic Layoffs

Further evidence of the interest of workers in the regulation of
and the protection from economic layoffs can be found in the
increase in the magnitude of these layoffs. In the period 1976–81,
economic layoffs increased by a rapid 80%, going from 203,754
workers in 1976 to 365,132 workers in 1981 (see Table 3–1). Not
surprisingly, the percentage of the laid-off unemployed out of the
total number of unemployed also increased, from 13.4% to 15.5%.
Along with the dramatic rise of unemployment because of the
expiration of fixed-term/temporary and interim employment,
the increase in economic layoffs represents the growing preca-
riousness of employment in France.

Table 3–1 records three types of economic layoffs: structural,
conjunctural, and bankruptcy. Structural layoffs are those that
follow or are part of the efforts of an employer to reorganize
production. They occur as the result of the installation of new
technologies or product lines, mergers, acquisitions, decentrali-
zation, or centralization. Conjunctural layoffs are those that are
prompted by forces outside of the control of an employer, such as
a loss of orders or market fluctuations. The bankruptcy figures
refer to those layoffs that occur as part of the insolvency, judicial
termination, or reorganization of a business. For the purpose of
compiling these figures, the Statistical Service of the Ministry of

Table 3–1   Economic Layoffs in France, 1976–1981

Type of Layoff	Number of Firms	Number of Workers Laid Off
1976/Workforce		21,316,800
Structural	9,281	25,833
Conjunctural	37,711	118,427
Subtotal	46,992	144,260
Bankruptcy	4,138	59,494
Total	51,130	203,754
1977/Workforce		21,443,200
Structural	11,923	32,578
Conjunctural	53,014	173,383
Subtotal	64,937	205,961
Bankruptcy	6,568	84,695
Total	71,505	290,656
1978/ Workforce		21,476,500
Structural	12,643	30,994
Conjunctural	54,000	171,863
Subtotal	66,643	202,857
Bankruptcy	11,185	117,838
Total	77,828	320,695
1979/Workforce		21,482,500
Structural	13,029	32,393
Conjunctural	47,596	143,446
Subtotal	60,625	175,839
Bankruptcy	11,238	96,032
Total	71,863	271,871
1980/Workforce		21,439,500
Structural	14,583	34,913
Conjunctural	59,401	158,442
Subtotal	73,984	193,355
Bankruptcy	13,455	116,166
Total	87,439	309,521
1981/Workforce		21,203,700
Structural	17,629	47,564
Conjunctural	79,503	210,159
Subtotal	97,132	257,723
Bankruptcy	10,845	107,409
Total	107,977	365,132

Labor puts each layoff in only one category—in practice, of course, these categories would overlap. Bankruptcy, as noted, might result in the closing or reduction of operations as well as in the reorganization of production; conjunctural conditions might lead to reorganization; and structural layoffs often result from attempts to anticipate or respond to an economic conjuncture.

There is little difference between the legal effect of structural and conjunctural layoffs. The delay prior to effecting the layoffs in order that the layoff plan can be submitted to the workers' representatives is two weeks to two months (depending on number of workers to be laid off) longer if the layoffs are deemed structural. The idea is that the employer would have more advanced knowledge of the necessity of the layoffs when they are part of a reorganization plan. There is a great difference between the legal effects of bankruptcy layoffs and other economic layoffs. The layoffs in the bankruptcy category are not subject to the administrative regulatory process (to be discussed later). While they must still be reported to the Ministry of Labor, these layoffs are totally under the control of the bankruptcy court and the trustee (*syndic*) appointed by the court to wind down or supervise the reorganization of the business.

The number of firms listed are those that have requested authorization for economic layoffs, either through the administrative or the judicial process. While there may be other economic layoffs that have occurred, they are illegal or have been nominally motivated by other than economic reasons (and this motivation has not been successfully challenged by the employee). There are no reliable data on illegal or improperly classified layoffs, but the numbers are probably significant among small businesses. It should also be noted that since the last half of 1981, the share of unemployment caused by economic layoffs has decreased—partly due to the tougher stance of the labor inspectors and the courts backed by the new Socialist government, and partly due to the attempts made to place temporary, interim, and part-time employees under the administrative regime.[5]

The Regulation of Economic Layoffs

The basis for the administrative regulation of economic layoffs goes back to legislation of the immediate postwar period and to the concern for a unified business–labor–government effort to rebuild the French economy. The Law of February 22, 1945 gave to worker-elected enterprise committees (*comité d'entreprise*) in each firm with 50 or more employees the right to be consulted in all matters affecting the size and structure of the firm's workforce. The Law of May 24, 1945 charged the minister of labor and his subordinates with the supervision of human resource allocation in the economy and specifically with the supervision of movements of personnel, hiring procedures, layoffs, and the enforcement of collective bargaining agreements.

Subsequent postwar governments and the courts quickly narrowed the scope of this legislation to collective layoffs for economic (as opposed to disciplinary) reasons. While the legislation required that employers receive authorization from the Ministry of Labor for layoffs, it did not specifically make the layoffs invalid if they were carried out without either application to or authorization from the ministry. Under these circumstances, the administrative procedure was generally ignored and soon abandoned. Between 1945 and 1967, the personnel of the Inspection Division of the Ministry of Labor decreased despite an enlargement of the division's role in mediation and conciliation.[6]

Since 1967, and particularly since 1969, the picture has changed. The personnel of the Inspection Division has more than doubled since 1967. The Socialist government has augmented both the number and training of the inspectors, particularly with regard to the supervision of economic layoffs. The sources of the present regulation of economic layoffs are labor accords as well as legislation. The controlling Law of January 3, 1975 is often characterized as a law negotiated among labor, management, and government. It takes the two-phase approach of the National Labor–Management Accord on the Stability of Employment (February 10, 1969) and its renewal by the Amendments of November 21, 1974, with certain important limitations to be discussed below.

The Consultative Phase

The first phase of the process is the consultative phase. It involves a consultation between a workers' representative and the employer before the layoff takes effect. The extent of this representation depends on the size of the enterprise concerned, the authority of the firm's chief executive, and the magnitude of the layoff.[7] In firms of less than 11 employees neither a workers' representative nor a consultation prior to a layoff for economic reasons is required by law. In enterprises of 11 to 49 employees, there are elected workers' delegates (*délégué du personnel*) who must be consulted prior to the employer's demand for administrative authorization of the layoffs.

In firms of 50 or more employees the law requires an elected enterprise committee that must be consulted prior to invoking the administrative procedure. In enterprises of 50 or more employees and more than one establishment, the law requires the existence of a central enterprise committee and separate establishment committees for each location. Whether the central enterprise committe must be consulted prior to invoking the administrative procedure depends on whether the layoffs affect more than one establishment and whether the chief executive of the affected establishment has primary authority over the layoffs.

The application of the consultative procedure also depends on the number of layoffs foreseen. The Law of January 3, 1975 applies the procedure to layoffs of ten or more employees effectuated within a 30-day period. In enterprises of less than 50 employees, the workers' delegates must be consulted at a duly-called meeting held prior to the demand for administrative authorization. Where an enterprise has 50 or more employees, the enterprise or establishment committee must be consulted at a meeting held before the request to the administration. The mandatory time lapse between the consultation and the submission of the demand to the Inspection Division varies from eight days to three months, depending on the number of layoffs and whether there is agreement or disagreement between the enterprise committee and the employer with regard to the provisions for those laid off.

Under the accords, if 50 or more layoffs are contemplated and there is disagreement between the enterprise committee and the employer, the dispute must be submitted to a labor–management mediation commission (*Commission Paritaire de l'Emploi*). Submission to this commission increases the waiting period before the administrative demand but does not require that the demand await a resolution by the commission.

While none of these consultations are required by law to have any specific content, the courts have suggested that they must be meaningful in the sense of providing a free exchange of views on the essential elements of the workforce reduction. The duty to consult does not imply a duty to bargain with the enterprise committees, workers, or unions. This latter duty may be implied, however, by the Auroux Laws (1982), named for the minister of labor who authored them. For the first time in France, this set of four laws mandated a duty to bargain annually over wages and working conditions.[8]

The Administrative Approval

The second phase of the process involves administrative authorization by the Ministry of Labor. The employer's demand for authorization of the layoffs must be in writing and include the following information:

1. The name, address, and phone number of the employer.
2. The nature of the operations of the enterprise.
3. The name, nationality, sex, date of birth, address, position and qualifications of each worker to be laid off.
4. The dates of employment of the affected workers.
5. The nature of the economic, financial, or technical reasons for the layoffs.
6. The actions undertaken to reduce the number of layoffs and to facilitate the reemployment of the workers to be laid off.
7. A schedule of the layoffs.

After receipt of the demand, the local director of the Ministry of Labor or his or her delegates (the labor inspectors) have 7 to 30 days, depending on the number of layoffs, to investigate and authorize or refuse the demand. If the layoffs are authorized or the time period expires without a refusal, the employer may proceed with the layoffs. If ten or more layoffs within a 30-day period are requested, the director has 30 days to make the decision. If less than ten layoffs are contemplated, the director has seven days and may take another seven days if the employer is notified in writing before the expiration of the first period. In the case of ten or more layoffs, the director is charged with verifying that the consultative measures were properly undertaken, that the economic justification of the layoffs is real, and that methods of minimizing the layoffs and their effects have been considered and implemented where economically reasonable. In the case of fewer than ten layoffs, the directors must only appraise the reality of the economic justification.[9]

It is important to note that, unlike the previous accords, under the Law of January 3, 1975 layoffs resulting from bankruptcy, judicial liquidation, or reorganization were excluded from the administrative process. While the local director of the Ministry of Labor must be informed of such layoffs, they are not subject to his or her approval or rejection. This excludes about one-third of all economic layoffs from administrative consideration.[10]

The Ministry of Labor is likewise charged with seeing that the selection of persons to be laid off conforms to the considerations mandated by law. These considerations are the family responsibilities, the seniority, and the quality of the employee's work. A collective bargaining agreement may specify the weight to be given to each of these considerations as long as they are all given some weight. Under the law, the employer is the sole judge of the skill needs of the establishment and of the quality of an employee's work. In the absence of the collective bargaining agreement, the employer may determine the weight to be given to each consideration.

Implementation

Once the layoffs are authorized, the employer may proceed to implement them according to the schedule submitted in the request for authorization. Layoffs that do not take place within the scheduled period, unless good cause for a delay is shown, are invalid. The layoffs do not become effective until the employee receives notification in writing by certified mail. An employee with at least six months seniority at the establishment is entitled to one month's notice or one month's wages. Employees with more than two years' seniority are entitled, in addition, to severance pay of at least one month's wages.[11]

An employer who has been authorized to lay off employees for economic reasons becomes subject to controls over the hiring of new employees, over layoffs for noneconomic (usually disciplinary) reasons, and generally over the movement of personnel in the establishment. For twelve months following the implementation of economic layoffs, an employer must request authorization from the Ministry of Labor for any new hiring and new layoffs, whether or not they are for economic reasons. Furthermore, the employer is required to report all movements and changes of personnel at the establishment.

These controls can often be burdensome and intrusive. They are officially intended to assure that the economic justification of the triggering layoffs was indeed legitimate, that later noneconomic layoffs are not really concealed economic layoffs, and that rehiring priorities are observed. Unofficially, these requirements can be used by the ministry as a lever to encourage the rehiring of laid-off workers and to negotiate a reduction of the originally proposed layoffs without the necessity of formally refusing the request for authorization.[12]

The French legislative scheme does not declare the invalidity of layoffs that violate the law unless those layoffs are of protected personnel (usually union officials and representatives of the workers). Only for these personnel may a court order rehiring if they have been laid off in violation of the law. Others who are laid off illegally have only two avenues of recourse: suing for damages or filing criminal complaints against employers who intentionally and willfully violated the law. The damage suits may be brought before specialized labor courts with panels of lay judges elected by employers and employees. The employee may be represented by his union.

If an employer laid off employees without seeking authorization, after authorization was refused, or without a real economic justification, those employees are each entitled to their actual damages including back pay with a minimum recovery of about $800. The criminal penalties of $100 to $1000 per violation are generally not imposed in substantial amounts and only in cases where the employer was well aware of the violation.

If the employer requested authorization and received it but did not observe all of the requirements with regard to notice, consultation, or implementation of the layoffs or if a valid economic justification was not present, the employees are each entitled only to their actual damages with no minimum recovery. This is generally a minimal sum and does not function as either adequate compensation to those who have lost their jobs or a deterrent to the violation of the regulations governing layoffs.[13]

Employment Policies and Workforce Reduction in Industrial Corporations

Policies of Large Corporations

The impact of the layoff regulation can be seen in the policies of firms faced with the need or the desire to reduce employment.

This impact must be judged, however, in light of two important factors. One is the condition of economic crisis in which France has existed to varying degrees since 1974 and which has impelled many firms to reduce their employment. The second factor is that French personnel management had remained, at least until 1974, paternal and geared to the formation of a stable workforce as part of the long-term growth of the firm. This second factor works in the opposite direction from the first; that is, it makes French employers somewhat more reluctant than their U.S. counterparts to resort to layoffs for reducing their workforce. The result is that since the economic crisis of 1974–75, large corporations have moved to reduce, restructure, and make more flexible their utilization of a stable workforce. At the same time, there has been an effort to achieve these goals without resorting to layoffs.[14]

Although the large corporations showed a net reduction of employment between 1968 and 1980, prior to 1974 all of the corporations (excluding those in textiles) increased or maintained their workforce. From 1974 to 1980, more than half of the corporations reduced their workforce by between 6% and 24%. Here again the watershed of the economic crisis of 1974–75 is evident.[15] These large corporations fell into three groups:

1. Corporations in industries such as textiles, construction, steel, and electro-mechanics (none of which were experiencing rapid growth) reduced their workforce by more than 10%. The number of layoffs was largely a function of the extent of employment reduction by attrition.
2. Corporations in industries where some activities were growing, such as chemicals and nonferrous metals, were able to maintain stable employment and could avoid layoffs (at least theoretically) by transferring employees to growth activities.
3. Corporations in objective economic circumstances similar or superior to those of the second group resorted to massive layoffs for the purpose of restructuring their workforce— often resorting to temporary workers or subcontractors in order to more easily respond to changes in markets and technology.

Between 1975 and 1981, even as economic conditions began to improve, the large corporations resorted more and more often to reducing their stable workforce, and more and more of these reductions were accomplished by layoffs.

Methods of Workforce Reduction in Large Firms

Hiring Freezes. The method of reduction the least burdensome to employees is a hiring freeze with reliance on attrition. For several reasons, however, this method proved unsatisfactory for large reductions. Turnover is extremely low, especially during periods of high unemployment, often approaching zero exclusive of deaths and retirements. Secondly, the cessation of hiring entails the aging of the workforce, often reducing productivity especially in assembly-line productions. Finally, a hiring freeze and the reliance on attrition takes no account of the need for the replacement of employees with special skills or for the need to change the skill mix of the workforce. For these reasons, hiring freezes are provisional or temporary tactics used for short-term difficulties or as a prelude to a more drastic workforce reduction.

Mandatory Retirement. To further encourage turnover, large French corporations have been lowering the mandatory retirement age. While most set the age between 60 and 62 so that employees can benefit from the government funded retirement security plan (ASSEDIC) (which guarantees a maximum of 80% of the employee's gross salary at the time of retirement), more and more large corporations are resorting to early or anticipated retirement plans. In these plans, the company must carry more of the benefit burden or else the employee receives less before reaching the normal retirement age. Typically, these plans guarantee 70% of the employee's gross salary beginning at age 56 and rising to 85% at age 60. Government financing of anticipated retirement is available for companies preparing to lay off workers for economic reasons. This latter provision was one of the modifications sought by business in the laws regulating layoffs. These early retirement plans may be regarded as the laying off of older workers. Many of the plans are not voluntary, but even where they are voluntary, the worker knows that refusal may cause a layoff with fewer benefits.

Voluntary Departures. Anticipatory retirement plans are but a subcategory of the general class of voluntary departures. In order to encourage workers to quit, many large companies resort to lump-sum severance payments usually in excess of 40,000 francs (approximately $4000). The willingness of workers to accept these payments decreases with the deepening of the economic crisis and the increase of unemployment in the region. The workers to whom these payments are most attractive are often the youngest and most skilled who are sure of obtaining other employment. When the offer of these payments is made known, the morale in the establishment often suffers greatly. For these reasons, "encouraged voluntary departures" have not been able to resolve more than 15–25% of the problem of workforce reduction for the large industrial firms in France.

Several of the large industrial firms have attempted to encourage the geographical mobility of workers threatened by workforce reduction. These efforts work best where the geographical displacement is not too great, where the new and old positions are comparable in skill requirements and benefits, and where the company further demonstrates its commitment to the worker by providing training for the new job and financial assistance for the move. Where these conditions have been met, whole establishments have been phased out with large-scale transfers of employees and no or few layoffs. Needless to say, it is rare for these conditions to be met in their entirety, so that seldom more than 25% of the workers threatened with layoffs have accepted transfers when offered. Furthermore, even under the best of conditions, the transfers seem to produce only the semblance of mutual satisfaction of the firm and the worker. The vast majority of transferred employees leave their new place of employment within six months.

New Jobs and Rehiring.   Finally, in the attempt to avoid layoffs, some large corporations, generally with the aid of the national and local governments, have attempted to develop new jobs in the vicinity of the establishment. The corporation attempts to move some of its other operations to the locality affected, to encourage the development of subcontractors in the area, and to aid existing small businesses with orders for goods and services needed by the large corporation. In addition, the large corporation will provide training to employees for the new jobs and limited wage supplements to employees taking lower paying jobs. Large corporations may also contribute to the financing of new businesses for the locality by providing loans.

Such a mode of avoiding layoffs is evidently very costly and very uncertain and, therefore, not widely pursued. Where major efforts have been made, the number of employees actually rehired in the newly created jobs rarely exceeds one-third of those affected by the workforce reduction. In the Nord-Pas-de-

Calais mining region (including such cities as Lille, Roubaix, Turcoing, Douai, and Denain) where the phasing out of coal mining caused a major reimplantation effort, the overall result was negative. The only successfully implanted businesses appear to be small automobile parts and assembly plants that have hired only a small number of the out-of-work miners—and these at greatly reduced wages and benefits.

Licenciement en Douceur.   While no *one* of these methods of workforce reduction appears to be extremely successful, in combination they have helped to avoid many outright layoffs and have provided benefits to the worker in excess of those available to the laid-off. They constitute what the French call methods of *licenciement en douceur* or "soft layoffs." Resorting to these methods of workforce reduction is an important way of avoiding the strictness of the administrative regulation and procedure for economic layoffs. It is important to note that these regulations help to protect employees not only through their specific provisions but also in encouraging corporations to consider their employees' (as well as their own) needs in a time of economic crisis, corporate restructuring, and workforce reduction. This is not to say that strict regulation has no negative effects on workers— these will be discussed later in the chapter.

Violations of the Regulations.   The administrative layoff regulations and procedures provide a standard by which the performance of enterprises in reducing their workforces can be categorized. Three general groupings can be distinguished. The first constitutes those firms, almost always small and closely held, that simply violate the law with respect to economic layoffs. These violations most often take the form of failing to notify the Labor Inspection Division of the Ministry of Labor about the layoffs as required. Such employers often try to claim that the layoffs were not economic, but disciplinary, and therefore not governed by the administrative procedures. This has also become a practice of some larger companies such as Talbot, the automobile manufacturer. In a two-year period, the Talbot plant at Poissy laid off nearly 2500 persons for reasons of discipline, insubordination, or incompetence. Although many of these layoffs were found to be illegal, the company was still able to reduce its workforce by over 1700 without resorting to the administrative procedure for economic layoffs.[16]

Other employers make the required notification, but do not

observe the employee consultation procedures or the mandatory
waiting periods. Often, they do not provide accurate information
about the extent of the layoffs and the possible alternatives to it.
Many small employers use the economic layoff procedure for
attempting to rid themselves of union militants.

The large industrial corporations are generally found in the
other two groupings. About one-third of them, and this group is
growing, resort extensively to the formal layoff procedure and
merely observe the law and provide the minimum of consultation, information, and time that the law requires. Aggressive
union action with the support of an aggressive labor inspector can
still reduce the number of layoffs and soften their impact on the
affected workers, but in general the enterprises in this category
proceed with their original plans, laying off the workers originally proposed and providing only those benefits required by
law.

When faced with major reductions in their workforce, most
large corporations have proceeded by some combination of the
methods for *licenciement en douceur,* avoiding layoffs even at
the cost of retaining unwanted workers. They have acted in this
way generally for four reasons: to avoid the intervention of
governmental officials and administrative inflexibility, to maintain morale among the workers remaining in the corporate workforce, to avoid restrictions on the hiring of new employees at the
affected establishment (new hiring is monitored by the Labor
Inspection Division afer the approval of economic layoffs), and
to avoid tarnishing the corporate public image. (Small- and
medium-sized firms are about equally distributed among the
three categories.)

Several factors seem to correlate with the type of workforce
reduction policy a large corporation employs. Paradoxically,
those corporations hardest hit by the crisis are most likely to
follow a policy of *douceur.* These corporations are most likely to
produce materials used in other production processes—metals,
chemicals, textiles, synthetics, etc. They generally have a long
history of ties to a particular locality and often are the major
employer in the locality. Unions are usually strongly implanted in
these industries; thus, massive resistance to layoffs, with full
community and official support, is a real possibility for such
firms. This latter factor, in conjunction with the restrictions in the
law, is probably the strongest influence on the type of workforce
reduction policy employed by the corporation.

Policies of Small- and Medium-Sized Firms

Through the first half of 1981, large French industrial corporations resorted to the administrative layoff procedure with increasing frequency. In 1981, approximately two-thirds of firms with 200 or more employees laid off workers for economic reasons. Less than half of these large firms resorted to layoffs in 1977. While large firms have had a slightly decreasing share of employment since 1974, they have had a steadily increasing share of economic layoffs. These firms are twice as likely to layoff as part of a reorganization of production than are smaller firms. Despite these statistics, an employee of a firm with 200 or more employees is less likely to be laid off than an employee of a smaller firm.[17]

This does not tell the whole story of the employment policies of large firms versus small- and medium-sized firms. Many of the firms with less than 200 employees are owned by or affiliated with large firms. To see the significance of this relationship and to grasp its impact on plant closings as well as economic layoffs, we will refer to research done on a sample of 180 industrial plants that laid off 10 or more employees for economic reasons in 1980. The plants were in the Ile-de-France, Bretagne and Rhône–Alpes regions.[18]

The layoffs at these establishments fell into three categories. In the first were the layoffs due to immediate financial difficulties— lack of orders, lack of capital, and loans coming due at a time of low cashflow. Such layoffs can be considered truly conjunctural. Forty percent of the establishments, generally those with less than 200 employees, laid off workers under these conditions. In 80% of these cases, the layoffs came at the beginning of a liquidation of the business (a plant closing).

The second category included a quarter of the establishments surveyed. It consisted of layoffs linked to a reorientation of production to better defend a market position, a merger of production units, or the abandonment of operations considered insufficiently profitable. In 60% of these firms, the layoffs were accomplished through a plant closing. Two-thirds of the establishments in this category belonged to larger French or foreign corporations.

About one-third of the firms studied, of which 70% belonged to larger enterprises, fell into the third category. The layoffs in this group were linked to a change in the management of the workforce and a change in personnel policy. This refers to such things as the greater use of subcontractors, more temporary and/or part-time employees, the intensification of work coupled with the laying-off of existing "permanent," often older, full-time employees. These layoffs did not accompany a closing, but often accompanied attempts by the employer to oust union militants and to demand wage, benefits, and work rule concessions from the remaining employees under threat of more layoffs. Immediate economic pressure to reduce the workforce was not evident in these cases, but employers used a generally bad economy as a justification for the layoffs and changed policies that would serve to destabilize the workforce and institute what the French call American style employment policies.

The sample was small, representing about 3% of the establishments in the three regions that had laid off 10 or more employees in 1980. Nevertheless, the study reveals another aspect of the importance of large firms in laying off for economic reasons that is not revealed in the Ministry of Labor's layoff figures: 40% of the establishments in the study, although small- or medium-sized themselves, were dependent on larger firms. Furthermore, 20% of the establishments in the study laid off workers as part of a plant closing.

As we have seen, large firms play an important role in layoffs and plant closings; thus, the layoff regulations have a great effect on these firms. Further evidence of their impact has come since a strengthened Inspection Division has been encouraged to scrutinize requests for economic layoffs more closely. Since 1982, economic layoffs and plant closings have accounted for a decreasing proportion of workforce reductions and unemployment. This reduction was accompanied by an initial increase in unprotected forms of employment (temporary, fixed-term contracts, and manpower subcontracting). These too have been submitted, at least partially, to the jurisdiction of the labor inspectors and layoff regulations.

It is clear that layoff regulations have had a substantial impact on the job security of French workers. The government, the employers, and the unions have also recognized this impact in a back-handed way. At the behest of the employers, the government encouraged negotiations between the national union confederations and the employers' association to work out some flexibility in employment relations and workforce management to meet market fluctuations. The confederations have withdrawn from these negotiations with the CFDT (Confédération Française Democratique du Travail), suggesting that such negotiations might be entered into at the industry level while the CGT (Confédération Générale du Travail) and the FO (Force Ouvrière) preferred to rest on the rights they have acquired under the law.[19]

Interpreting the Legislation in Light of Its History

A full understanding of the impact of the layoff regulations and the role myth and power play in that impact cannot be obtained without looking at the legislative and social history of the regulations in France. Three landmark dates in the development of the administrative procedure for economic layoffs give rise to the idea that the procedure was designed to facilitate layoffs and head off greater restrictions after periods of turmoil and worker militancy.

1945 to 1969

The Laws of February 22, 1945 and May 24, 1945, which established formal rights and procedures for notice, consultation, severance pay, and reemployment, were a direct response to both the need for labor's cooperation in the rebuilding of France and the central role of socialists, communists, and trade unionists in the resistance.

While some of the architects of these laws foresaw a comprehensive rationalization of human resource allocation, at the urging of employers the courts narrowed their authority to regulating (and thereby sanctioning) layoffs for economic reasons. The early promise of this legislation blunted the demands of workers for a more collaborative role in the postwar economy and for greater guarantees of security. With the decline of militancy and the removal of the left from postwar governments, the legislation soon fell into disuse.[20]

The second landmark date is May–June 1968 when an uprising, which was furthered by the wildcat strikes of young workers and eventually joined by the trade unions, resulted in the Grenelle Protocol. The protocol, negotiated under the wing of the DeGaulle government, raised wages, authorized union organization at the plant level, and promised greater worker participation and job security. Following the protocol and a worsening of

France's balance of payments, employers and unions negotiated the National Accord of February 10, 1969, on the security of employment.

This accord, which revived the administrative procedure for economic layoffs and provided substantial benefits for the laid-off, was welcomed by employers worried about continued worker militancy in hard economic times and about upcoming salary negotiations. The substantial benefits negotiated, and underwritten by the government, allowed the unions to suppress the demand that young workers had formulated during the wild-cat strikes of May–June 1968: "No layoff without the prior approval of the enterprise committee and the guarantee of an equivalent new job."[21]

The major union confederations and the employers all wanted this accord negotiated at the national level. After suffering severe blows to their progressive image among young workers and the public during the May–June uprisings, the union confederations wished to establish their legitimacy as "social partners" with employers and the government. The employers wished to avoid bargaining at individual plants because they feared local militancy would wrest even greater protections and rights for workers from individual firms. The national-level negotiations, removed from local militancy, tended to be concerned with the detrimental effects of new benefits and rights on smaller firms, thereby reducing the final scope of these benefits.[22]

The 1970s

The 1974 extension and amendment of the Accord of 1969 and the adoption of the Law of January 3, 1975 took place in a period of turmoil. The period between 1974 and 1975 was marked by pervasive strike activity, especially wildcat strikes led by younger workers, along with a new form of militant labor action. In the LIP Watch Company and the Pechiney–Noguères strikes, the strikers illegally occupied the plants, barred management from the premises, and continued production on their own. This action touched off a wave of similar strike tactics, and support of the strikers became a major political issue in the 1974 election, which was only narrowly lost by a coalition of left parties. The LIP strike had begun over plans to sell the French company to a large Swiss conglomerate. This new militancy was a reaction to what seemed to be the unfulfilled promises of 1968 and 1969 and to the growing concentration and transnationalization of French industry linked to layoffs and closings.[23]

One of the first acts of Giscard-d'Estaing's government on June 21, 1974, was to convoke the unions and the employers and urge them to enter into an agreement on job security and the improvement of working conditions. The government itself raised the guaranteed minimum income, social security, and family allowance payments. In convening the negotiations, the government warned that if no agreement were reached by October 30, it would have to act unilaterally.[24]

The October deadline passed. The employers, buoyed by the election victory of the right and hardened by the economic downturn, sought a reduction of delays and penalties in the layoff procedure. The unions, spurred by a new found militancy evidenced by the wave of worker occupations of plants, saw the employer's proposals as a return to the previous unenforceable reliance on the 1945 legislation. The CGT and the CFDT wanted a guarantee of equivalent placement for each worker laid off as well as a greater range of inquiry for the work inspectors. They also wanted more severe penalties and longer delays in the layoff procedure. The FO supported these latter measures but was willing to compromise them.

On November 19, partly in support of a two-month-old postal workers strike, but also as a show of strength to influence the on-going negotiations on job security, a one-day, nationwide general strike was called by the CGT and the CFDT. The effect of the strike was inconclusive. On November 21, the CNPF (Confédération Nationale du Patronat Français), the association of employers from large enterprises, and the FO reached a compromise agreement that essentially continued the provisions of the 1969 agreement. The association of small employers, the CGT, and the CFDT did not sign the agreement.[25]

The dissatisfied unions then turned to the government, demanding that it make good on its election promises and on its promise at the convening of the labor negotiations. The unions wanted legislative action to put more force into the layoff regulations so they would protect all workers. The resulting legislation, the Law of January 3, 1975, is often spoken of as a "negotiated law." It enacted into law, thereby extending to nonsignatory parties, the bulk of the recent renewal of the 1969 agreement. In addition, the legislation established civil and criminal penalties (noted above) for employers who failed to observe the requirements for economic layoffs. It required that employers consult annually with enterprise committees as to the evolution of employment within the firm. Employers were required to consider and to implement where possible measures for the reemployment of workers affected by layoffs.

In the end, however, the law appeared to the CGT and CFDT as a public relations effort covering up a contraction of the workers' rights gained in the agreement of 1969. The new law limited the time period for the decision on authorizing layoffs to a maximum of 30 days. The earlier agreement had allowed for indefinite extensions of this period. In the debate over the new law, the National Assembly—on the advice of the government—rejected an amendment that would have allowed the delegates of the workers to see all the information upon which the request for layoffs was based. The assembly's conservative majority also adopted an amendment excluding layoffs that resulted from a judicial liquidation or reorganization from the purview of the administrative procedure.

The conservatives hammered away at creating the public image of progressive legislation. The Gaullist chairman of the legislative committee that had proposed the restrictive amendments declared:

> *This legislation is one more step in the direction of a goal yet distant, that which we will reach when workers benefit fully from the moral and material rights which have always been theirs and are less and less contested everyday. One great reform remains to be accomplished: the reform of the enterprise itself.*[26]

To highlight their dissatisfaction with the proposed legislation, the CGT and the CFDT staged one-hour, national work stoppages and a mass demonstration in Paris on December 12, 1974—two days before the final vote in the National Assembly. In the final vote, the legislation was adopted by a wide margin. The Communist party abstained and the Socialist party voted against it. The employers and the conservative government, with much public fanfare about reforming the corporation and giving workers new rights, had succeeded in masking the restriction of previously acquired workers' rights and powers of government intervention in both the negotiated extension of the Accord of 1969 and in the legislative process as a whole.

An Interpretation of the Interplay of Law and Power

Given this legislative history, it is possible to view the Law of January 3, 1975 as an example of the power of business interests to control the legislative agenda and to pass off as progressive reform what is actually a restriction of workers' rights. This view portrays the law more as an instrument for regularizing and facilitating layoffs and for supervising the optimal allocation of the workforce than as a measure for job security. Even the earlier agreements and provisions for special unemployment benefits to those laid off for economic reasons seem more than anything else to be an effort to buy off labor militancy at the lowest possible cost to flexibility in the restructuring of enterprises and the management of the labor force. This view is evidenced also by the ministerial circulars and court decisions demonstrating a restrictive interpretation of the power of the labor inspectors.

The new law, unlike the previous agreements, did not mention the avenue of collective negotiations or the Bipartite Commissions for resolving continuing disagreements as to the necessity, extent, and conditions of economic layoffs. This was certainly in keeping with the post-1974 goals of the CNPF to limit negotiations, forestall government intervention, and marginalize the trade unions.

This view of the legislation seems further supported by the low rate of formal refusals of authorization for layoffs—3-5% of the layoffs requested annually in the period between 1977 and 1982. The labor inspectors themselves, at least prior to 1982, have shared this perspective, noting that they were discouraged from aggressive investigations by their lack of time, personnel, training in financial matters, and support from higher-ups. Several inspectors interviewed recalled cases in which the decision to refuse layoffs was reversed by departmental directors or by the minister of labor, and the inspector who had issued the refusal found him or herself sitting at a desk, isolated from colleagues, without any cases (despite a shortage of personnel).

Aside from such informal but direct pressure, the law provides for only a limited inquiry into the existence, not the substance, of the economic reasons for the layoffs. There is no provision for the assistance of an independent accountant. In addition, economic layoff procedures trigger relatively high unemployment benefits capable of reducing the resistance of workers to the layoffs, while transferring the cost to the public treasury. By excluding layoffs consequent to a judicial liquidation or reorganization from the administrative procedure, the Law of January 3, 1975 places approximately one-third of all economic layoffs beyond the reach of the labor inspectors.

In the face of this evidence that employers had used the law to facilitate layoffs while trying to maintain a progressive image, it might well be said that French workers, despite their more radical analysis of the capitalist system, have fared no better politically than American workers in fighting layoffs and plant closings. This runs counter, however, to the evidence discussed above that the layoff regulations had caused firms to avoid layoffs whenever possible and had resulted in government and business sponsored schemes for "soft layoffs."

In attempting to resolve this contradiction, it is necessary to look at three ways in which the administrative process actually operates. In approximately one-half of the cases under their jurisdiction, the inspectors intervene actively and, at some point during the process, refuse to authorize 30% or more of the layoffs initially proposed. These refusals do not always result in the ultimate cancellation of the layoffs, but they always lead to a reconsideration and delay of the planned layoffs.

Secondly, the instances in which an inspector finds that a proposed economic layoff is in fact an attempt to dismiss worker representatives or militants are not included in the refusal statistics. Usually, such a situation is settled by the withdrawal of the request rather than the refusal of the inspector to authorize the layoff. In this way, the administrative process can help to preserve the resistance of the workers to the layoffs.

Thirdly, the law, despite its deficiencies in this regard, requires that the employer inform and consult the workers' representatives as to the number of layoffs, their economic justification, and the procedure by which they will be carried out. Since the administrative process comes into play most often after information or consultation either has not taken place or has not resulted in a negotiated settlement, its aggressive use provides a time, forum, and impetus to the parties to negotiate. The incentive for the employer to negotiate is created by the power of the inspector to refuse or greatly delay the layoffs. Rather than lessening trade union and worker resistance to the layoffs, the procedure is strongly and positively correlated with that resistance. The more aggressive the inspectors, the more militant the workers—and vice versa. Furthermore, aggressive action by the inspectors and/or the workers tends to expand both the political and geographic extent of conflict leading to the possible intervention of the departmental, regional, or national government and the industry level of the trade unions. This expansion means a greater likelihood that negotiations will take place, that the layoffs will be prevented (or surely delayed and diminished in number), and that the position of laid-off workers will be improved as to rehiring, retraining, and benefits. When the conflict is expanded, the local community tends to benefit from concessions made by the enterprise and from governmental aid.

The administrative procedure is not a hindrance to labor militancy and resistance to layoffs. In many cases, it provides crucial time and information for massive resistance to the employer's layoff project. In other cases where massive resistance is not feasible, the procedure can move the parties to negotiate a settlement of the conflict. The legislation provides only the potential for, not the assurance of, such use and then only when coupled with militant workers and sympathetic and aggressive labor inspectors.[27]

A good example of a major, but indirect, effect of the requirement that the enterprise committee be given notice prior to layoffs or a closing is the conflict surrounding the United French Tanneries in Annonay. While the notice requirement did not prevent the closing of the tanneries, it did help to delay that closing and provided the time for a successful popular mobilization and public effort to reopen them. This is partly what those in the United States who oppose advance notification requirements wish to avoid.

The mobilization included the occupation of the plant and the town hall and a demonstration in Paris. The coalition that formed with the aid of the CFDT and CGT to combat the closing of the tanneries raised the dispute to a new level when it helped the parties of the left (most of whose candidates were union and coalition members) capture the local and regional governments from a conservative group that had been entrenched for over fourteen years. The new public officials immediately began an innovative and successful program of industrial revitalization and job creation.[28]

The Role of Myth and Power

The employer's economic power and its underlying legal props form the foundation of the myths of big labor, the business climate and legality in France as in the United States. French workers and their unions anticipate the failure of certain demands and suppress those demands before they become public issues. Postwar prosperity and economic growth have also given rise to versions of the myth of big labor and the myth of legality. The latter, however, are of more recent origin than in the United States and are countered by a strong working class, anticapitalist orientation that robs them of some of their power over political action. Olivier Kourchid, sociologist and keen observer of the labor scene, studied responses to the economic crisis of 1974. He found that "workers do not in general accept the traditional explanations of the economic crisis. . . . [T]hey identify two types of causes: the anarchy and incoherence of the capitalist economy and, concurrently, the repression and exploitation of the worker by the corporations and the rich."[29]

All three major French trade union confederations oppose capitalism in principle. Kourchid and two of his colleagues found that this doctrinal opposition between the employers and the unions hardens during times of economic crisis. Labor demands are more prone to focus on the economic decisions of the enterprise and on those areas that management sees as their domain, such as investment and the organization of production. Negotiations take place only at the national level, impasses are frequent, and disputes are often resolved by legislation.

Because confederations are bulwarks of the Socialist and Communist parties in France, when a left-wing government is in power, unions expect that their anticapitalist orientation is shared and that they will have a major influence on economic and industrial policy. Their demands for legislation are radical—calling for nationalization, investment controls, total security of employment, and worker participation in management. While the measures demanded of a left government are radical, the expectations of support for these measures from the government lead to a decline in the political mobilization and pressure applied by the unions. When a government of the right is in power, as has been most often the case in recent French history, the demands are less radical (responding to the second face of power, the power to suppress) but the pressure applied is often greater.

These tendencies clearly relate the political demands of the labor movement and the jurisdictional level at which action takes place. In good times, despite militant rhetoric, there is an "everyone for him- or herself" approach. Both employers and the unions emphasize negotiated settlements at the enterprise level and seek to avoid government intervention and national accords. The subjects of negotiation are most likely to be salaries, benefits, individual employee grievances, and shop floor conditions. When production slows, the unions attempt to consolidate the gains they have made during good times; job security becomes an important issue; and employers are less willing to bargain unless they can exchange some minor monetary concessions for industrial peace in the face of workforce adjustments. This tends to create impasses at the local level that push disputes and negotiations to the national level where the government is likely to take a hand.[30]

Faced with governments of the right and with the durability and domination of the capitalist system, workers have generally acceded to the second face of power by moderating their anticapitalist political demands in the context of collective bargaining.[31] At times when great political change seemed imminent, such as in 1936, 1945, 1968, 1974, and 1981, these demands for nationalization, workers' control, etc., were made public issues, only partially addressed, and eventually suppressed. Most recently the third face of power (myth internalized) and the myth of big labor have been demonstrated in the dashed expectations of radical change that followed the Socialist victory in May of 1981.[32]

The Enterprise as a Community:
Differing Views from the Top and the Bottom

Despite the tendency of French workers to analyze their economic situation in radical terms, blaming capitalism and employers, the hidden face of the employer's power still works in subtle ways. The myths of big labor and the business climate tend to be expressed as different views of the "enterprise as a community." One view considers the enterprise as the place where the workers form strong social bonds and where they assert their collective power in creating a community that serves their human, as well as economic, ends. This is a form of the myth of big labor. The other view is that workers owe allegiance to the enterprise whose interests are economic and whose activities are determined by the owner and management.

Hugues Puel, labor economist and head of the research institute, Economie et Humanisme, has suggested that in the present hard economic times, the myth of the enterprise can no longer be maintained. Puel notes that French workers have come to regard employment in terms of the following six criteria, all of which are becoming less certain even as they become more fixed in the public consciousness.[33]

1. The establishment of an employee relationship is connected to a particular business or institution from which one receives a regular monthly salary.[34] In this context, the employee is distinguished from the self-employed or the independent contractor or artisan on the one hand, and on the other hand, from the temporary, hourly, or seasonal employee. The French refer to the ensemble of employee relations and working conditions inside the firm as the social climate; that is, the connection of the employee to the firm is widely regarded as forming a type of community established by a "social contract." The unions and the employers are similarly called "social partners." (It must be remembered that the French term for business corporation is *société*.)

2. Employment must be stable. This entails regular hours, the maintenance and improvement of job skills, a regular progression in salary and in responsibility, and continuity in the relationship of the tasks performed during a working life. This could be designated as the expectation that a job will be a career.

3. Employment is full-time. The employee expects to spend a substantial part of each day at work, participating in the work community in which he or she has substantial ties.

4. One job will be the principal source of revenue for the worker. Workers expect that they will earn enough from their employment to support themselves and their families in a

decent manner without depending on second jobs and other
sources of revenue (such as government benefits, inherited
wealth, rents from land, or ownership income).

5. A worker, after some early job changes, will have one
   employer during his or her worklife, thereby further enhanc-
   ing the communal nature of work ties.
6. Employment is tied to a specific workplace (an office, a lab,
   a factory, or a shop) that is separate from the home and
   provides a stable base of operations, accountability, and
   social relations for the worker.

Economic crisis and the reshaping of the structure of employment in France, as in the United States, has exploded this myth of
employment, making employment possessing the criteria outlined above unattainable for a large and growing segment of the
population. The result is great frustration and confusion for the
worker who finds that his ideal of employment is a myth. The
result is not, despite a radical analysis of the causes, a more
combative stance on the part of the worker.

Kourchid found that the more insecure employment became
(i.e., the more it departed from the myth) the lower the level of
labor/management conflict in the firm. He noted that "as the
employment conditions of the worker and his mates worsened,
their alienation increased and their vision of the crisis shortened.
Rather than increasing solidarity and collective action at the
enterprise level, there was a tendency to look to the national
unions and the government as the parties responsible for avoiding
layoffs and aiding workers. Ony where great worker solidarity
preceded the crisis was militant local action in the face of employment insecurity likely to occur.[35]

This phenomenon, as well as the effect of the employer's use of
its version of the myth, is evident from the following example of a
light bulb factory (François-Lyon), part of an electrical goods
firm affiliated with International Telephone and Telegraph
(ITT). The 700 employees had fought unsuccessfully to prevent
short hours and partial unemployment over an eight-month
period. At the end of that period, the company announced the
possibility that the factory would be closed or that there would be
extensive layoffs. At the time, ITT was negotiating with Philips to
sell the factory. Several workers at the factory were interviewed,
and they all commented on the extensive propaganda campaign
conducted by the company to emphasize the profundity of the

economic crisis and its responsibility for the short time and
layoffs. While the workers did not accept this argument, it had left
them confused and uncertain as to what tack to pursue. Some of
their comments follow:[36]

> *Martine: I am pessimistic. The coming months will not be easy. It
> will be necessary to fight to get anything, if we want to save ourselves,
> save our factory, and save the other factories in the company. It's the
> only thing to do if we don't want to let them get rid of us and close
> us down.*

> *Jean: It's the worry. Everything is happening so quickly. The threat
> is immediate. At the moment, there are the negotiations with Philips,
> our filament shop is already closed. Anyway, Philips doesn't need us.*

> *Liliane: Me, I'm with my friend, Martine. I am as pessimistic as she.
> I don't see much of a future.*

> *Alain: We are trying now to have some informational meetings on
> the future of the company. We wonder what we can do in the context
> of the crisis. If we fight at the level of the company where there are
> 2300 of us, how can we make a multinational conglomerate like ITT
> listen, especially with a government that is not interested in labor
> problems? We hear that there are presently 200 factories occupied
> [by their workers], some for more than six months, but that's not even
> mentioned in the press. That's why we are somewhat discouraged
> about what we are able to do. In ordinary times, we'd know how to
> fight. But now, we wonder what to do. Ineffectiveness, from the
> union's point of view, means no future and we are not optimistic
> about the future of this company.*[36]

Employers, represented by CNPF, purveyed the myth that the
enterprise was a community. They emphasized their role as the
undisputed head of that community and the preeminent status of
the economic goals of that community. Not until 1968 did employers recognize the right of unions to organize and bargain at the
plant level. As late as 1965, the president of the CNPF said: "We
will never allow the penetration of trade union activities into the
enterprise. This can only be imposed upon us by force."[37] This
proved prophetic. It took the uprising of May–June 1968 and the
resulting Grenelle Accords of 1969 to obtain official recognition
of trade union rights at the enterprise level.

Under threat of legislative intervention, the employers encouraged negotiations at all levels between 1969 and 1974. François
Ceyrac, then secretary of the CNPF and later president, declared
this new policy: "We are more and more convinced that it is the

plant level negotiations which alone have the power to suitably resolve the problems that legitimately preoccupy the workers as well as the government." The economic crisis and the collapse of the left-wing electoral challenge, however, brought a return to earlier policies and attitudes with which the employers had always been more comfortable. As president of the employers' organization, Ceyrac himself stressed the liberty and autonomy of the enterprise embodied in its chief executive, the avoidance of corporate reform through legislation, the struggle to marginalize trade unionists in the enterprise, and the limitation of collective bargaining.[38]

The employers generally have the power to set the agenda for corporate and labor policy—the trade unions can at best react. This was evident in the legislative history as well as the implementation of the French layoff regulations. It reflects the fact that although there is strong, conscious opposition to the power of capital, the hidden faces of power are still effectively linked to the power over economic resources. The reaction of workers and trade unions in a hostile environment requires that they make their case in the economic terms appropriate to the capitalist economy. This in turn increases the role of myth.

Rank and filers, although accepting the radical analysis of their situation, are confused not only by the raw power that they face, but also by the need to address that power in its own terms. Such confusion saps militancy and strengthens the tendency to look to the national confederations, the government, and established legal forms to deal with problems that directly affect the worker's environment. This increases the power and autonomy of the employer at the local level where any changes in the work process must eventually be implemented. It also distances the worker from direct involvement in collective actions to influence the production process.

Since 1981, the lack of militancy at the local level has been translated into a lack of political pressure on the Socialist government, which, like all governments in power, tends to respond to pressure. In addition, the French version of the myths of big labor and legality gave workers and unions the expectation that the mere election of a Socialist government, supported by labor constituencies, was enough to counter the power of capital. During a period when workers and unions should have mobilized at all levels for negotiations and political action aimed at increasing job security and worker participation and at decreasing the number of hours worked per week, they largely sat back and waited for the government to do their work for them.

The wait and see attitude of workers encouraged employers to seek flexibility in the management of their workforces by using the law, avoiding the law, and at times breaking the law. Employers used the law by taking disputes with the workers and the labor inspectors to the courts, which were always more sympathetic to employers. They avoided the law by resorting more often to unprotected forms of employment and by closely supervising and documenting employees' minutest errors or disciplinary infractions in order to dismiss them for cause. They broke the law by firing people without invoking the required consultations or receiving administrative authorization and by firing, transferring, and isolating militant workers and union representatives.

While the government tried to resist these moves, it finally gave in to the myth of the business climate. Without strong pressure from the workers, the government could not resist the threat that employers would simply not invest and would transfer their capital elsewhere if prolabor measures were not curbed and if an austerity program designed to decrease consumption, salaries, and benefits were not imposed. Government economists gave the myth of the business climate an interesting twist. They argued that French economic growth must be slowed because economic growth increased consumption, and increased consumption would increase imports—thereby worsening the balance of payments and the competitive position of French industry. While the workers were not convinced, they were confused and frustrated by the adoption of the myth by "their" government.[39]

Recommendations Reevaluated

To a large extent, the recommendations made in Chapter 2 seem to be borne out in the analysis of the French plant closing and layoff regulations. Periods of militancy have brought major political and economic successes to French workers. When their militancy has lapsed at crucial moments, failure has often resulted. The uprisings of 1968 brought substantial labor law reform including the initial accord that established layoff regulation. The widespread strikes and factory occupations of the early seventies, even in a time of economic recession, brought concessions from employers. At the local level, the administrative controls on layoffs are most effective when workers pressure their employers and the authorities. The case of Annonay is a good example of the favorable political and economic fallout from worker militancy. When workers ease their pressure, even on a Socialist government, they are no longer regarded as an equal "social partner."

A recent study has indicated that, even in large firms with highly developed bargaining structures, partial and total work stoppages are often essential in order to reach an agreement considered favorable to workers. Total work stoppages of long duration are more effective in achieving favorable results than partial or short-term stoppages. Militancy pays off.[40]

Unionization, solidarity, and increased union services to members and nonmembers go together. French unions each see themselves as representing the working class; that is, all workers and their families. They provide services to all of these groups and are very concerned that benefits won by the union be extended to all workers. Labor unions own vacation colonies, assist in the management of social security funds, deal with housing problems, and provide training and educational activities. French unions are "cultural" organizations in that they concern themselves with all aspects of a worker's life. Trade unionists remain members of their unions even after retirement or layoff.

While the actual dues-paying membership of trade unions is about 22% of the French workforce and has declined in recent years, the elections for lay members of the labor courts show that 80% of French workers support one of the three major trade union confederations rather than independent or management-sponsored unions. Because French unions need not represent a majority at the workplace to have a legally recognized presence or to negotiate an agreement and because workers remain members of the union even after they no longer work for a firm in the industry, layoffs and plant closings do not reduce membership as drastically as they do in the United States.[41]

French unions have only a very small number of paid professional employees or full-time officials. At the local level, the work is done almost entirely by volunteers who are, by statute and collective agreement, guaranteed a certain amount of work time for union activities (as are all employees). Dues are also voluntary. Local leaders are generally the most militant unionists and must keep close contact with their coworkers and members. Because they do not always have a majority of workers as members of their union in a given plant or facility, they must often convince nonmembers and members of other unions to take collective action. To maintain an effective presence at the enterprise level and to collect dues, the national confederations and unions must, and generally do, support the most committed and militant workers when they take action.

Political unionism has proved successful for French workers, but this has also created some problems. While the unions and the national confederations have striven to separate their leadership from the leadership of the political parties and to define a political role for themselves that is different from that of the political parties, the major confederations were unable to refrain from closely identifying themselves with the coalition of left parties in the elections of 1974, 1978, and 1981. As previously noted, this led to a state of euphoria after the election of 1981, which left strictly labor relations activities as well as political activities in a state of neglect. Furthermore, because of the close identification of some of the leaders of the largest confederation, the CGT, with the declining French Communist party, the CGT has been the victim of red-baiting and charges of authoritarianism.

As the case of Annonay and the case of Longwy in the next chapter suggest, French labor unions have been somewhat successful in generating the local support, especially in working class and mono-industrial communities. This local support has often been instrumental in obtaining results from the layoff regulations and from strikes and occupations. In these communities workers and labor unions have a positive image, although they face some of the same problems as American unions in capturing the support of younger generations. Neither television nor the schools, despite heavily unionized staffs, have regularly conveyed an image of the strengths of the labor movement and working class. As in the United States, even among union members, fewer and fewer French workers share the industrial working class values out of which unions were born. To the extent that unions have grown, it has been among immigrant workers, government employees, teachers, and office and service workers. French unions have been only slightly better than American unions in reaching out to immigrants, women, and the young.

Their anticapitalist orientation has assisted French unions in two ways. First, it has attracted many white-collar intellectual workers in education, government, and even business. Second, it has provided alternative myths and political programs with which to combat the myths and programs that are detrimental to workers' interests. As the next chapter will show, the anticapitalist orientation has encouraged, at least since 1978, more and more instances of proactive economic planning by unions rather than mere reaction to plans formulated elsewhere. This has proved to be an aid to mobilization. It has helped to avoid some of the confusion similar to that experienced by the workers in the light bulb factory.

Endnotes

1. The statistics in this section are drawn from Sérvices des Etudes de la Statistique, *Statistiques du Travail: Bilan de l'Emploi 1981* (Paris: Ministère du Travail, 1982), pp. 15–17 and *Statistiques du Travail: Bilan de l'Emploi 1982* (1983), pp. 15–34; "Quand la France se compte," *Le Monde*, sélection hebdomadaire, Feb. 16–22, 1982, p. 10.
2. *Statistiques du Travail* (1982), pp. 20, 40, 49; *Statistiques du Travail* (1983), pp. 105–10. The protections to which "permanent" and temporary employees are entitled will be discussed below.
3. *Statistiques du Travail* (1982), pp. 32–36.
4. *Statistiques du Travail* (1983), pp. 105–10; "Les experts de l'OCDE préconisent un 'assouplissement' de la rigeur en Europe," *Le Monde*, sélection hebdomadaire, May 30–June 5, 1985, p. 9.
5. "Rapport sur les droits des travailleurs," *Liasons Sociales: Documents*, no. 125/81 (Nov. 2, 1981), pp. 4–5 and from interviews with labor inspectors and union officials.
6. M. Bacot, L. Foucher, M.-F. Mouriaux and M.-M. Orhand, "La Législation sur les licenciements: son application dans un contexte de crise économique," *Cahiers du Centre d'Etudes de l'Emploi*, no. 16 (1978), p. 244; Claude Chetcuti, "Les licenciements économiques: la pratique administrative," *Droit Social*, no. 2 spécial (Feb. 1978), pp. 29–31.
7. Here again it is important to distinguish between an establishment and an enterprise. An establishment is a facility at which operations are at a single geographic location and closely related to each other. An enterprise is generally defined as a unity of legal ownership or practical control that may itself own or control several establishments.
8. The 1945 law, now Art. L.432–4 of the Labor Code, and the Accord of 1969 require that enterprise committees be generally consulted within a "reasonable time" prior to any reduction of the workforce. This would include the laying off of even one employee. The failure to observe these provisions is not considered grounds for administrative refusal of the layoffs. Furthermore, in the case of a single layoff for economic reasons, the worker concerned is entitled to an interview with the employer prior to the demand for

administrative authorization. Here again there is no specific waiting period after the interview, Pierrette Rongère, *Le Licenciement* (Paris:Les Editions Ouvrières, 1977, 1980), pp. 140–51. The Auroux Laws include the Law of August 4, 1982, the Ordinance of February 1982 and the Decree of September 10, 1982. The rights of temporary, fixed-term and interim employees are established primarily in the latter two laws.

9. The Council of State (Conseil d'Etat), the highest French court for administrative law, has defined the verification of the "reality" of the economic justification as confirming that the employer's reasons were in fact based on a plausible appraisal of the economic situation of the enterprise. The council clearly indicated its disapproval of second-guessing the employer on the optimal management of his business, while charging the administration with preventing employers from using economic reasons as a pretext for ridding themselves of employees they disliked for other reasons—decision of April 27, 1979 in the case of the *Coopérative laitière du Puy.*

10. *Liasons Sociales: Controle de l'Émploi et Licenciement Economique,* no. spécial (March 1981), pp. 24–37.

11. Ibid., pp. 40–41.

12. Ibid., pp. 8–13.

13. Ibid., pp. 55–56.

14. C. Beauvialla et al., *Les Stratégies de Structuration de l'Émploi des Grandes Groupes Industriels,* 6 vols. (Grenoble: Institut de Recherche Economique et Planification-Developpement, 1979). vol. 6, p. 69—this study of 17 large industrial corporations covers the period from 1968 to 1980.

15. The following analysis of employment policies comes largely from Bernard Soulage, "Les politiques d'emploi dans les groupes industriels," *Sociologie du Travail,* no. 1 (Apr.–June 1981), pp. 134–48.

16. Tiennot Grumbach, "La gestion disciplinaire: Le droit de l'apparence," *Travail,* no. 5/6 (Nov. 1984), pp. 46–79; Anne Mayère, "Une petite ville exsangue," *Economie et Humanisme,* no. 263 (Jan.–Feb. 1982), pp. 40–45.

17. The statistics that precede and follow are from *Statistiques du Travail,* note 1 (1982), pp. 40, 71 and (1983), pp. 123–38 and from other unpublished data of the Sérvices des Etudes Statistiques of the Ministry of Labor. The definitions are from the *Bilan de l'Emploi,* note 1 and from *Liasons Sociales: Controle de l'Emploi et Licenciement Economique,* note 10, p. 16.

18. The research was carried out by the Travail et Société research group. The report of the research is found J.-Y. Boulin, "Le système français de rélations industrielles face aux licenciements économiques," in *Rapport Final Action Programme DGRST: Conflits et Négociations* (Paris: Travail et Société, 1981), pp. 66–97.

19. Alain Lebaube, "L'augmentation des emplois précaires pourrait expliquer la baisse du chômage," *Le Monde,* sélection hebdomadaire, May 23–29, 1985, p. 9; Alain Cédel, "La conjuncture économique et financière," *Economie et Humanisme,* no. 281 (Jan.–Feb. 1985), pp. 96–97. The major labor confederations in order of size of reported memberships and performance in the labor court elections are the CGT or General Labor Confederation, the CFDT or Democratic French Labor Confederation, and the CGT–FO or the General

Labor Federation–Workers' Force. The CGT is most closely associated with the Communist party and the left wing of the Socialist party. It claims about 2,000,000 members, a high proportion of which are in large firms and heavy industry. The CFDT is more closely associated with the Socialist party and a large proportion of its 600,000 members are teachers and white-collar workers. The FO, stressing its political independence, claims about 600,000 members, a high proportion of which are in heavy industry. It also has a high proportion of members from executive and supervisory ranks, who may join unions in France.

Each of the confederations is made up of unions which represent branches of economic activity such as metals, chemicals, trucking, education, etc. Each union has national, regional, and local levels. There are some smaller confederations and independent unions, see generally Jean-Daniel Reynaud, *Les Syndicats en France* (Paris: Seuil, 1975); Jacques Rojot, "A New Chapter in French Industrial Relations," in Solomon Barkin (ed.), *Worker Militancy and its Consequences* (New York: Praeger, 1983), pp. 312–23.

20. See generally F. Collin et al., *Le Droit capitaliste du travail* (Grenoble: Presses Universitaires de Grenoble, 1980); Bernard Edelman, *La légalisation de la classe ouvrière* (Paris: Christian Bourgois Editeur, 1978); compare Karl Klare, "Judicial Deradicalization of the Wagner Act and the Origins of Modern Legal Consciousness, 1937–41," *Minnesota Law Review*, 62 (1978), pp. 265–339.

21. "Le patronat et les syndicats se mettent d'accord pour indemniser les travailleurs victimes des concentrations industrielles," *Le Monde*, Feb. 8, 1969, pp. 1, 21; "L'accord sur l'emploi et la révision de la procedure de discussion des salaires du secteur public peuvent améliorer le climat social," *Le Monde*, Feb. 9–10, 1969, pp. 1, 14; "Les réactions des syndicats," *Le Monde*, Feb. 12, 1969, p. 29; Claude Chetcuti, note 6, pp. 29–39.

22. Jocelyne Loos, "Accord de contenu ou accord de méthode?" *Sociologie du Travail*, no. 1 (Jan.–Mar. 1983), pp. 15–31.

23. "L'emploi déjà," *Le Monde*, June 11, 1974, p. 1; Gérard Terrieux, *LIP: C'est fini?* (Paris: unpublished thesis, University of Paris I, 1980).

24. "M Chirac préside la rencontre patronat–syndicats destinée à préparer la seconde phase du plan social," *Le Monde*, June 21, 1974, pp. 1, 37, 38.

25. "La 'grève nationale'," *Le Monde*, Nov. 19, 1974, p. 1; "Trois accords, un même objectif," *Le Monde*, Nov. 29, 1974, p. 32.

26. "Le projet de loi sur les licenciements collectifs prévoit une pénalisation des sociétés," *Le Monde*, Nov. 29, 1974, p. 33; "La CGT et la CFDT estiment que le projet de loi sur le licenciement n'est qu'une opération publicitaire," *Le Monde*, Dec. 12, 1974, p. 42; "Les deputes adoptent le projet de loi sure les licenciements collectifs," *Le Monde*, Dec. 14, 1974, p. 40.

27. J.-Y. Boulin, "L'inspecteur et les licenciements économiques," *Actes*, no. 31/32 (May–June 1981), pp. 32–36; Bacot, et al., note 6; Cecelia Casassus and Sabine Erbes-Seguin, *L'Intérvention Judiciare et l'Emploi: Le Cas du Textile* (Paris: Documentation Francaise, 1979); Chetcuti, note 6; J.-P. Bachy, *Administration du Travail et Conflits Collectifs* (Paris: Centre de Recherches en Sciences Sociales du Travail, 1979). Recent improvements in

the powers, training, and personnel of the Inspection Division and the creation of an Economic Research Service along with more encouragement from higher-ups since the accession of the Socialist administration have resulted in a more aggressive control of economic layoffs. Layoffs and plant closings have been reduced since 1981.

28. Bernard Ganne, "Conflit du travail et changement urbain," *Sociologie du Travail*, no. 2 (April–June 1983), pp. 4–17.

29. Olivier Kourchid, *Crise Économique et Modes d'Action Ouvrière: Récherche Exploratoire sur la Vulnerabilité de l'Emploi et les Comportements Ouvriers dans Trois Branches Industrielles en 1975* (Paris: Comité de Recherche du Diplôme d'Etudes Supérieures, 1976), p. 282.

30. Sabine Erbes-Séguin, Cecilia Casassus, and Olivier Kourchid, *Les Conditions de Developpement du Conflit Industriel* (Paris: Groupe de Sociologie du Travail, 1976), pp. 21–28.

31. Alain Lebaube, "Le chômage a deux régimes," *Le Monde*, sélection hebdomadaire, Feb. 9–15, 1984, p. 7; Alain Cédel, "La conjuncture économique et financière," *Economie et Humanisme*, no. 283 (May–June 1985), pp. 74–75; Michel Noblecourt, "La négociation sociale est–elle encore possible?" *Le Monde*, sélection hebdomadaire, May 16–22, 1985, p. 8; but see, Guy Herzlich, "La CGT réaffirme son opposition à 'une politique de casse' industrielle," *Le Monde*, sélection hebdomadaire, May 9–15, 1985, p. 7. Similar views were also expressed in interviews with officials of the CGT, CFDT, and FO in Paris, Aix-en-Provence, Longwy, and Marseille.

32. Michel Noblecourt, "L'entreprise au coeur du dialogue social," *Le Monde*, sélection hebdomadaire, Apr. 4–10, 1985, p. 9; Eric Le Boucher, "La fin du dogme des nationalisations," *Le Monde*, sélection hebdomadaire, Apr. 25–May 2, 1985, p. 7; Jacques Le Goff, "L'expression des salariés, deux ans après: propos d'étape," *Economie et Humanisme* no. 283 (May–June 1985), pp. 51–61.

33. Hugues Puel, "Le paradigme de l'emploi," *Analyse, Epistemologie, Histoire*, no. 18 (Dec. 1979), pp. 2–8.

34. Since April 1970, as a result of a national accord supported by the government, an increasing proportion of French workers have received salaries on a monthly basis rather than hourly wages, Jean-Daniel Reynaud, "France: Elitist Society Inhibits Articulated Bargaining," in Barkin (ed.), note 19, pp. 285–88.

35. Kourchid, note 29, pp. 282–88.

36. D. Gones, *Silence, On Ferme! Les Licenciements Vus par la Base* (Paris: Les Editions Ouvrières, 1976), pp. 49–50.

37. Jean-Pierre Maindive, *Les Politiques Patronales d'Amélioration des Conditions de Travail* (Aix-en-Provence: Institut Regional du Travail, 1981), App. p. 3.

38. Ibid., App. pp. 9–10.

39. Alain Vernholes, "Un nouveau plan de rigueur à l'horizon 86?" *Le Monde*, sélection hebdomadaire, May 23–29, 1985, p. 9; François Grosrichard, "Le gouvernement veut attirer les investissements étrangers," *Le Monde*, sélection hebdomadaire, June 13–19, 1985, p. 8; Michel Noblecourt, "La déprime des syndicats," *Le Monde*, selection hebdomadaire, Feb. 28–Mar. 6, 1985, p. 8.

In 1984 four major nationalized industries—steel, automobiles, coal mining, and ship building—have announced in conjunction with the government a plan for the reduction of employment. The companies and the government have, under pressure from the unions, pledged that they will force no layoffs. To this end, the government on February 8, 1984 proposed a plan for encouraging early retirements at age 50, for negotiated reductions in working hours compensated in part by the government, for retraining leaves at 70% of pay for up to two years, and for benefits to those who take other jobs at less pay. This plan also includes the creation of regional centers for the development of small and medium-size enterprises with government loans and subsidies. These centers correspond, with one exception, to regions especially hard hit by reductions in employment of the four major industries noted above. "Le plan gouvernemental de modernisation," *Le Monde*, sélection hebdomadaire, Feb. 9-15, 1984, p. 6; "Les restructurations un an après," *Le Monde*, sélection hebdomadaire, Mar. 15-20, 1985, p. 11.

40. Sami Dassa, "Conflits ou négociations? Les grèves, leurs résultats et la taille des entreprises," *Sociologie du Travail*, no. 1 (Jan.–Mar. 1983), pp. 32–44.
41. Solomon Barkin, "Summary and Conclusion: Redesigned Collective Bargaining Systems in Eras of Prosperity and Stagnancy (sic)," in Barkin (ed.), note 19, p. 242.

Chapter 4

CONFRONTING MYTH AND POWER: YOUNGSTOWN AND LONGWY

This chapter will compare the opposition to plant closings in the steel industry at Youngstown, Ohio, and at Longwy, Lorraine. In so doing we shall see if very different strategies were influenced by differing responses to the myths of big labor, the business climate, and legality. The responses to plant closings and work-force reduction in the steel industry at Youngstown and Longwy provide an illuminating comparison of how myth and the hidden faces of power influence forms of struggle and how elites use their power to prevent or inhibit challenges to their control of decision making. In particular, we shall be interested in whether or not the power of myth over human minds acts to stifle or contain the political and economic demands of subordinate groups and the forms of action by which the groups try to realize their demands.

We examine who accepts or rejects the myth of big labor or the belief that labor's power over business and politics is excessive and should be reduced. This myth can lead to the refusal of workers or unions to challenge investment decisions or economic policy because they feel unqualified to do so. On the other hand, the workers can reject this myth but still be affected because it is accepted by the public and government officials. The accep-tance of the business climate myth can have a similar effect in that it prevents challenges to the economic analyses put forward by business and to the claim that any interference with the interests of capital is detrimental to the public interest. Finally, the acceptance of the myth of legality can exclude a whole range of tactics that were instrumental in the founding and earliest successes of the labor movement.

The rejection of the myths by workers and their unions opens up new forms of struggle but, at the same time, can force elites to alter their methods of struggle and to use the full gamut of their powers with devastating effect. Thus, at both Youngstown and Longwy, the struggles revealed the shared interest of government and capital in suppressing workers' claims for a voice in industrial policy, and in both instances, the restructuring of the steel industry went forward despite the opposition.

Similarities in the Struggles at Youngstown and Longwy

Before delving into the differences that distinguish the two cases, it is important to outline some of the similarities that make the comparison of Youngstown and Longwy instructive. Both are working-class "steeltowns" of central and long-standing importance to steel-producing regions. Youngstown, on the Mahoning River with the towns of Warren and McDonald to the north and Campbell and Struthers to the south, was the site of 21 blast furnaces by 1875. Over the years more than one-fifth of the area's employment has been in primary metals. Longwy, near the Belgian and Luxemburg borders, anchors the north end of a string of smaller towns, half of whose working population has been directly employed in iron and steel making for at least five generations. Both Longwy and Youngstown depend on rail and truck transportation for raw materials and the shipping of their products. From 1977 to 1980, Longwy and Youngstown each suffered the loss of over 10,000 jobs in the steel industry (this constitutes one-third to one-half of the local employment in that industry) along with the complete or partial closings of several steel plants. Furthermore, the reductions in the local steel industry workforce have not been halted—in both towns, further steel employment reductions are planned.[1]

The fight to preserve steel industry employment in both Youngstown and Longwy faced some similar obstacles. Both regions have an early history of militant and even violent labor actions in the steel industry. Between 1905 and 1906, there were

several confrontations between striking miners and steel workers
and troops in the Lorraine. In 1915, conditions in the steel industry
gave rise to a strike and riot that culminated in the burning of East
Youngstown (now Campbell) and the calling of the National
Guard. The Youngstown area was also the site of some of the most
militant "little steel" strikes of 1937.

The post-World War II period in both communities began with
strikes: the 1946 strike in Youngstown and the bitter strikes of
1947–48 in Longwy. Following these strikes and lasting until at
least the late 1960s there was a period of relative quiescence
caused by increasing wages and the growing assurance that steel
was not just another industry but a necessity for national independence and prestige. This bolstered important aspects of the
business climate myth: the belief that the steel industry would
inevitably grow and that the growth would ensure well-paid jobs
for present and future generations. Even the French steel workers
of the Lorraine, militant trade unionists, and Communist party
supporters, who intellectually rejected the ideology behind the
myth, were lulled into a false sense of confidence in the growth of
the private economy as the guarantor of their employment.

The mythic status of the steel industry and the effect of that
status in obscuring reality was well described by Yves Agnes in *Le
Monde* at the time the last of the wave of closings was being
carried out in Longwy:[2]

> *Steel is at once a myth and a mystique. It is the symbol of power and
> prosperity. The nation sees itself in its steel industry, whose interests
> are confounded with the national interest.... This belief is not to be
> discussed. It is thus for the leaders of the majority as for the opposi-
> tion, for the trade unions, the media and public opinion.*

The following analysis of the place of steel in the world economic debate is even more dramatic:[3]

> *He who smelted this metal became equal to the gods: thus believed
> the Bedouins of Mount Sinai, convinced that he who makes a sword
> of molten iron becomes invincible and is assured of victory over his
> opponents.... What is there really behind all of the ideological dis-
> cussions of our contemporaries? What is there, if not the extraordi-
> nary magical-religious prestige of iron and the neolithic myths which
> survive in the form of institutional and ideological symbols?*

Youngstown workers put their shock over the steel closings in
more concrete terms. "The only thing I can compare it with is

Pearl Harbor," said one worker describing his feelings to an ABC film crew. Another recalls, "Most people couldn't believe it. It was so huge and had operated so long and so many people depended on it for their livelihoods." A militant French worker too, at least at the gut level, responded with shock to the destruction of his version of the myth of the business climate, the myth of the enterprise as a community: "We have worked so hard. They can't do this to us!"[4]

The myth of legality and the myth of big labor created another obstacle to worker militance at both Youngstown and Longwy. The United Steel Workers of America (USWA), representing most of the workers in the closing plants, had long had supplemental unemployment benefits in their union contracts. These benefits, as noted in Chapter 2, promised a substantial proportion of the workers' wages for their first year of unemployment. The workers laid off in the closings of the Campbell and Brier Hill Works were also deemed eligible to receive Trade Readjustment Assistance. While these benefits were provided in full to those who were victims of the earlier layoffs, the depletion of the Supplemental Unemployment Benefits (SUB) reserves and the cutbacks in TRA funding and eligibility caught those laid off later by surprise. Workers laid off from the United States Steel Corporation (U.S. Steel) plants learned only belatedly that they would not be eligible for TRA.

The benefits available to workers immediately following the closings were apparently ample for the first year. Many workers assumed that this would easily allow them time to find other employment equal to or better than their present jobs or that the steel industry would be recovering before their benefits ran out. Since these were benefits based on being laid off for economic reasons, militant actions (especially if illegal) could lead to disciplinary dismissal and a resulting cancellation of benefits. Frank Leseganich, Youngstown district director for the United Steel Workers, believed that the resistance to the closings would have been more successful if it had waited for the workers to "get hungry" after their benefits had run out. The workers at Longwy were also beneficiaries of a special unemployment regime. They were guaranteed 90% of their wages for the first year after being laid off along with substantial rights of transfer, early retirement, and job retraining. Furthermore, as resistance grew at Longwy, the government and the steel companies upped the ante by announcing even greater benefits and incentives to retire, transfer, or quit.[5]

In both cases, time was also an obstacle to resisting the plant closings. The longer the battle continued, the more depleted were the resources of the workers, the more deteriorated was the condition of the closed facilities, the less likely became the retention of the plant's previous markets, and the less public attention was paid to the struggle. Only if the struggle had resulted in an initial postponement of the closings, could these factors have been reversed. Even with such a postponement, the companies, with control over investment and sales, would have been able to allow the progressive deterioration of the facilities and markets of the doomed plants (as was certainly the case in both Youngstown and Longwy before the announcements of the closings). In any case, with their income in jeopardy, the seemingly large economic incentives offered, and the lack of a definitive success for the resistance, workers drifted away from struggle, if not from the region. One Longwy steel worker noted, echoed by many others, as the struggle drags on, "[o]ne thinks a lot of oneself. Solidarity? That doesn't last long."[6]

The final shared obstacle to successfully resisting the plant closings was the difficulty of reaching and pinning down the decisionmakers responsible for the closings. Neither Longwy nor Youngstown were the seats of power of the primary corporate or governmental actors. Lykes Corporation, owner of Youngstown Sheet & Tube, was based in New Orleans. Ling-Temco-Vought (LTV), which merged with Lykes just before the Brier Hill closing, is based in Dallas. U.S. Steel is based in Pittsburgh, and crucial board of directors meetings were held in New York City. The key governmental decisions affecting the Youngstown worker/community buyout attempts were made in Chicago (Economic Development Administration (EDA) regional office) and Washington, D.C. The crucial decisions affecting Longwy were all made in Paris. Furthermore, all of the key decisions were made in relative secrecy, closed to worker participation and announced amidst efforts to characterize the decisions as unplanned, but immediately necessary, responses to external economic forces.

The buck was being constantly passed from the corporations to the government and then back again. The corporations blamed the Environmental Protection Agency's (EPA) antipollution regulations and the Carter administration's failure to limit foreign

competition. The government passed the decision-making re-
sponsibility on redevelopment funds back and forth between the
Department of Housing and Urban Development (HUD) and the
Economic Development Administration of the Department of
Commerce. In postponing decisions on the award of loan guarantees, the White House referred the Youngstown Ecumenical
Coalition back to Lykes for a firm price and conditions of the sale.
Lykes initially delayed making the commitments on the grounds
that the Justice Department had not yet approved the Lykes/LTV
merger and later because the approved merger had not yet been
completed. The action of the Justice Department in approving
the merger, against the recommendations of its own Anti-Trust
Division, changed the marketing basis on which the buyout pro-
jections had been made and required revised applications to be
made to HUD and the EDA.

The workers of Longwy were faced with similar maneuvers.
The government refused to engage in tripartite negotiations that
would bring together itself, the unions, and the steel companies.
They used separate negotiations to dilute responsibility and
heighten the workers' and the public's confusion about where
responsibility for the closings and job reductions lay. When the
minister of labor, Robert Boulin, agreed that the restructuring of
the industry would be suspended during the negotiations of
February–March 1979, the minister of industry, André Giraud,
announced that the restructuring plan was not suspended. When
the chief executive officer of Usinor, a major metals company,
agreed to postpone workforce reductions during the negotiations,
the chairman of the board announced that there would be no
postponement. When the CGT and the CFDT negotiators indicated that they were prepared to discuss only the restructuring
plan, not benefits, the minister of industry said that he had no
authority to discuss changing the plan. He referred the federations to MM. Etchegarray and Mayoux, the chief executive officers of Usinor and Sacilor–Sollac (another metals producer).
When the negotiators met with these executives, they stated that
they were required to follow the government's plan for restructuring because the government, in fact, owned the controlling
interest in the steel companies. Both the government and the steel
companies blamed the European Economic Community (EEC)
for requiring reduced French steel production.

The exclusion of workers, the secrecy, and the buck-passing
were accompanied by versions of the myths of big labor and the

business climate. Workers were said by governmental and corporate officials to be unqualified to participate in or question economic or financial decisions. Their attempts to intrude into these decision-making processes were considered unjustified burdens on the power of capital to pursue its interests which were deemed to coincide with the public interest. That this was the use of the myths for political purposes can be seen by the silencing or ignoring of knowledgeable people in government and the industry, such as the chief of the Anti-Trust Division of the attorney general's office or the director of the Usinor–Longwy plant, who questioned the analysis that led to the closings.

Lykes employees were threatened with "blacklisting" in the steel industry if they communicated with the media or community organizations about the closings. The fact that such threats were credible indicates that the steel companies formed a powerful network in opposition to the interests of the workers and the community.

Local executives seemed to have had no influence on the decisions made in corporate headquarters. Many, seeing the handwriting on the wall, resigned before the closing or shortly thereafter. William Kirwan, superintendent of the Youngstown Works of U.S. Steel, apparently presented several plans for saving the works to top executives and directors of the corporation. Yet, when the decision to close the works was made, the chairman of the board and the chief executive officer claimed that they had never heard of the plans. In Longwy, the powerlessness of the director of the Usinor plant was even more obvious. When he suggested that the company should keep the mills in Longwy open rather than build a new plant at Neuves–Maisons, he was dismissed.[7]

Differences Between the Two Struggles

Despite the similarities, the effort to preserve the steel industry proceeded very differently at Youngstown and Longwy. As one analyst suggests, "the modes of action and of mobilization seem to rest on institutional foundations diametrically opposed."[8] In Longwy, workers immediately took the lead in the struggle. They organized demonstrations, strikes, factory occupations, and sabotage. They mobilized both inside and outside the plants. With the aid of their national federations, they broadened the struggle to reach public opinion and corporate and governmental decision makers in Paris. They even set up their own radio stations to keep up the mobilization and inform the public of developments.

In Youngstown, outside of an initial petition drive that advocated the claims of the steel companies against the government, the major responsibility in the "Save Our Valley" campaign was undertaken by the Ecumenical Coalition—an organization of Youngstown area clergy. This effort was conducted entirely within the bounds of legality with the goal of obtaining government funds to achieve the worker/community buyout. Demonstrations, when they did take place, had disappointing turnouts. Only after U.S. Steel announced the closing of the Youngstown Works did workers step to the fore of the efforts to preserve the plants. Two short-lived occupations of U.S. Steel offices in Pittsburgh and in Youngstown followed. Litigation was a primary aspect of the workers' efforts against U.S. Steel. Until the very end of the battle, neither workers nor the Ecumenical Coalition received much support from the USWA headquarters. In fact, the initial efforts of the coalition were greeted with outright hostility and red-baiting by the USWA leadership.

A major difference in the two struggles was actually established prior to the announcement of the closings. The United Steel Workers of America had, at least since I. W. Abel's no-strike proposal of 1967, accepted the steel industry's analysis of its problems (foreign competition and environmental regulation)—the myth of the business climate. Under Abel, who also accepted the myths of big labor and legality, the union and management had created joint committees to discuss productivity improvements and new contract procedures. In the Experimental Negotiating Agreement of 1973 (ENA), adopted without rank and file approval, the USWA gave up its right to strike, even at the expiration of a contract, in return for binding arbitration on disputes and a $150 bonus for every union member.

In 1977, the election of Lloyd McBride to the presidency of the USWA, with the aid of the 70% of the members who were not in basic steel production, confirmed this trend. The defeated candidate Edward Sadlowski, who had gained a majority of the votes of the steel mill based membership, had been a long-time opponent of the ENA and of the USWA contract approval process that excluded rank and file participation. The cooperative relationship between the USWA leadership and the companies established prior to the Youngstown closings, as well as the union leaders' prime constituency, assured that the USWA would have no independent analysis or plan for steel industry development and basic steel job preservation.[9]

The situation could not have been more different in Longwy. At least since the economic crisis of 1974–75 and the 9% decline in world steel demand in 1975, the major trade union federations had opposed the EEC and national plans to reduce basic steel production and employment. For several months before the announcements of December 11 and 12, the CGT and the CFDT had been preparing detailed plans for the steel industry. In August, the CGT had requested that the government open negotiations on the future of the steel industry. Such direct participation in industry planning was a big new step for the unions. Despite their anticapitalist orientation, the French federations, like American unions, had had neither the research capabilities nor the will to engage in economic planning. This had been left to the political parties with which the federations were loosely associated.

In the summer and fall of 1978, the metal trades unions of both the CFDT and CGT began putting together their own proposals for the steel industry. They had four points in common. The first was the total rejection of government and company plans on the grounds that they ignored the national importance of the steel industry and that they merely aimed at the short-term restoration of profitability rather than a complete modernization and reintegration of steel production with upstream and downstream industries. The second point was the raising of production targets for the coming years. The projected increase in demand for French steel was based upon the third and fourth shared points. The third point was the increased efficiency due to the conversion to oxygen and electric furnaces and continuous casting with corresponding savings on energy and raw materials. The fourth and final point was a better orientation to the needs of the downstream industries both domestically and in less developed countries.

Both federations were constrained to make their arguments in terms of the capitalist economic assumptions under which the crisis was being managed by the government and the companies. They had to establish their credibility in the same terms as their interlocutors in order to hope for real negotiations and public support.[10]

The counterplans of the unions were an important factor in the mobilization of the Longwy workers and their communities when the closing announcements were made. First, they exposed the collusion and the failure of government and the companies to consult the workers or their unions on the restructuring plans. No longer could it be argued that such consultation was unnecessary because the workers lacked the expertise to deal with the complex structural reorganization of the industry. No longer could it be argued that the workers' reactions were merely emotional or ideological and not based on hard economic analysis. The explanation put forward by the unions for the failure to consult them was simply that the government, allied with capital, had used its raw power to avoid the questioning of its own shaky analyses.

Second, workers could mobilize *for* something as well as against it. They had their own proposals, based on sound economic analysis, for the preservation of the industry. Workers' responses to the question, "What is to be done?" echoed that of a Usinor electrician:[11]

> *Preserve the steel industry, modernize it in integrating its industrial markets, machine-tool factories for example.*

Third, the plans captured the public's imagination by emphasizing the importance of the steel industry to national economic independence. Likening the steel industry to the energy industry, the unions called attention to the effects of energy dependence during the oil crisis. The unions maintained that the government's plans would put France in the same vulnerable position with respect to steel. The unions were also in a position to profit from the steel myth noted earlier.

Finally, the plans were a bargaining tool. They served to require their interlocutors to react. This was usually the disadvantageous position in which the unions found themselves—reacting without sufficient preparation. While in the end the unions' plans did not prevail or clearly result in a change of the government's original plan, they served to force concessions on other issues. The arrogance of the government in not considering the union's plans was another factor in creating public support for the ousting of Giscard d'Estaing in 1981. Ironically, this brought in a government of the left that then proceeded to cut steel employment further.

The Onset of the Two Struggles

On September 19, 1977, which Youngstown came to know as "Black Monday," Youngstown Sheet & Tube, owned by the Lykes Corporation since 1969, announced that it would close the Campbell Works. This would cause 5000 layoffs, the first of which would begin the following Friday. In Longwy, successive shocks came on December 11 and 12, 1978. First Sacilor-Sollac and then Usinor announced the elimination of more than 20,000 jobs in the steel industry, including 15,000 in the Lorraine. This entailed the closing of all but one small part of the La Chiers plant in Longwy. The town of Longwy itself would lose 6500 steel jobs.

The first reaction of the workers in both Youngstown and Longwy was to get the local unions together to confer. The USWA locals met with District Director Leseganich on the day of the announcements. On December 12, the CGT convoked the interunion committee on which was represented the CFDT, FO, CGC (Confédération Générale des Cadres), and FEN (Fédération de l'Education National, the teachers' union) to formulate a joint response to the crisis.

The actions following the gathering of local unions diverged greatly. The Youngstown steel workers agreed on a petition drive. The petition was directed to the White House and it echoed the business climate myth of steel executives calling for environmental regulation waivers, foreign import quotas, and profit protection. Two hundred fifty steel workers brought these petitions, with over 100,000 signatures, to Washington on September 23—as the first laid-off workers left Campbell. At the same time, USWA district officers were meeting with local government agencies to assure benefits and services to laid-off workers. Testifying in Congress on the day after the closing announcement, USWA president, Lloyd McBride, agreed with steel executives that the industry layoffs were caused by steel imports.[12]

Symbolically, the first action at Longwy was the lighting of a neon sign declaring *"SOS EMPLOI"* (SOS EMPLOYMENT) atop a slag heap. The sign, which had actually been erected by the CFDT two days before the layoff announcements, was visible for several miles around. The interunion meeting of December 12 resulted in the planning of several mass demonstrations and labor actions. On December 19, 1978, 25,000 people demonstrated against the layoffs in the main square of Longwy–Bas; such a massive mobilization had never before been seen in the region. On December 20, 500 CFDT members occupied the meeting room of the enterprise committee at La Chiers to prevent the committee from being formally notified of the layoffs as is required by law. On the next day, Usinor workers streamed from the plant to demonstrate in Longwy. On December 22 CGT members occupied the chambers of the Metal Industry Employers Association. From December 23 to 25, the CFDT held a well-attended open house on the slag heaps for members of the community.

At the same time, small groups of workers were organizing and carrying out illegal "strike force operations" designed to attract attention to the plight of Longwy and to pique the national authorities whom they held responsible for the closings. For example, on the morning of the demonstration at Longwy-Bas, the CFDT and local truckers blocked the railroad tracks used to carry ore to the steel plants. On the next day, the Calais–Bâle and Paris–Luxemburg trains, carrying foreign steel products and iron ore, were bombed. From December 25 to 28, the interunion committee organized the blocking of all routes into Longwy and all routes to the Belgium or Luxemburg borders that passed in or near Longwy. CGT members occupied the Usinor offices at Senelle, and sequestered several executives on December 28.[13]

From the outset, actions at Longwy, under union leadership, took on a militancy lacking in Youngstown. Both at the local and the national level, the USWA abandoned leadership roles in attempting to preserve steel jobs in Youngstown until two years after Black Monday when U.S. Steel announced the closing of its Youngstown Works. Lloyd McBride, whose office was only 65 miles away, did not even pay a visit to Youngstown until seven months after the first shutdown announcement. Unemployed workers did not form their own organization to fight job reduction in the steel industry until March 1979. The 400 workers and family members forming Steelworkers United for Employment (SUE) turned to the Ecumenical Coalition rather than the USWA for startup funds. They committed themselves to supporting the coalition's worker/community buyout plan. Individual union members, particularly several officials from the Brier Hill Local #1462, were active participants from the start of the Ecumenical Coalition efforts, but union or worker participation, as the coalition itself admitted, was disappointing.[14]

Actors, Tactics, and Goals in the Struggle to Save Steel Jobs

Youngstown

The Ecumenical Coalition. From Black Monday until the EDA's final rejection of loan guarantees for Community Steel (the proposed worker/community owned company) on March 30, 1979, the Ecumenical Coalition was the principal actor in the Youngstown effort to save steel jobs. The origin of the coalition can be traced to a phone call on September 19, 1977, from the Cleveland office of Episcopal Bishop John Burt to Bishop James Malone, head of the Catholic diocese in Youngstown. The call was suggested by Reverend Charles Rawlings, the activist regional Episcopal staff person for church and society issues, who had read of the Campbell closing announcement in the afternoon paper. One week later, Bishop Malone organized a breakfast discussion with several other local clergy, Richard Barnet of the Institute for Policy Studies (IPS), a left–liberal thinktank, and Staughton Lynd, labor lawyer and left-wing activist.

Within two weeks, Bishop Malone, with the assistance of Reverend Rawlings and of Father Ed Stanton, Malone's staff person, was heading a coalition of clergy from most of the Youngstown Christian and Jewish congregations. Initially, the coalition expected to play a supporting role in the local business and labor communities. They formulated their role as one of articulating the moral and humane concerns arising from the plant closing and of helping public and private agencies respond to the needs of the laid-off workers and the community. As time went on and other potential actors seemed to evaporate, the coalition adopted a more activist position on the moral duty to preserve jobs. Taking such a position was strongly encouraged by Reverend Rawlings and Father Stanton and by their connections with Staughton Lynd, the IPS, and later Gar Alperovitz, economist and head of the Washington based National Center for Economic Alternatives (NCEA).

While the idea of buying the Campbell plant was suggested by Gerald Dickey of the Brier Hill local at a public meeting held in Campbell on September 25, the actual formulation of an action goal occurred at the Steel Crisis Conference called by the Ecumenical Coalition for October 28–29, 1977. That conference brought together leaders of the local, regional, and national church organizations and economic development experts. While the experts spanned the political spectrum, it was Gar Alperovitz who stressed the moral issues involved in massive unemployment and loss of professional status and thereby captured the imagination of Malone, Stanton, and Rawlings. It was these men who then became the prime movers of the religious coalition. The conference, during which the Ecumenical Coalition took on a formal structure, formulated a four-point action program.

The first point was local and national public education on the moral dimension of the Youngstown plant closings and economic disinvestment. The religious leaders proposed a "pastoral letter" identifying the moral issues and calling the community to action. The letter would appear in full-page ads in newspapers across the country. Second, the conference proposed coordinating efforts to assure that Youngstown viewpoints were heard in the formulation of a national steel industry policy with emphasis on the preservation of basic industrial jobs in smokestack communities. Third was obtaining the support of national church bodies for a Youngstown Project responding to the threat to employment and quality of life caused by plant closings. The fourth point was the creation of a task force to study the feasibility of workers and the community acquiring and operating the Campbell Works or, in the alternative, finding some other job-generating use for the property.[15]

Three activities dominated the coalition's agenda in November and December of 1977. The first was the drafting and circulating of the pastoral letter, which was publicly released on November 29 with the signatures of 240 clerics. The letter forthrightly condemned Lykes for a violation of ethical principles that even a corporation must follow. The second item was the initiation of a feasibility study of the reopening and modernization of the Campbell Works. The coalition worked with a local economic development agency, Western Reserve Economic Development Agency (WREDA), whose consulting engineer had access to Youngstown Sheet & Tube records. During November, coalition leaders met in Washington with HUD staff and with an undersecretary of the treasury to explore the possibility of grants and loan guarantees for buying, reopening, and modernizing Campbell. After initial favorable responses to all of these efforts, on December 12, 1977, the coalition publicly announced its intention to buy and reopen the Campbell Works. The quick and forceful action of the coalition resulted in an agreement with local political leaders and economic development officials to keep the coalition in the lead in negotiating federal aid for the worker/community buyout plan. This bore fruit on December 30, when the coalition obtained a $335,000 contract from HUD for Alperovitz and the NCEA to do a thorough feasibility study of the reopening of the Campbell Works in preparation for an Urban Development Action Grant application.

The Lykes/LTV Merger.   During November and December, it also became clear that Lykes Corporation (owner of Youngstown Sheet & Tube) and LTV (owner of Jones & Laughlin Steel) were negotiating a merger. The consequence of that merger would affect the coalition's plans in three ways. First, such a merger would surely result in the closing of the Brier Hill Works because Jones & Laughlin had a similar plant using a more modern technology only 40 miles away. This would in turn mean more unemployment and pressure to expand the coalition's efforts to include reopening the Brier Hill plant. Second, the merger also eliminated the most likely markets for Campbell's steel if the plant were to reopen because those markets would now be supplied by Jones & Laughlin facilities. Finally, the merged companies would remove the Campbell coke furnaces for installation in their other mills, leaving Campbell without a necessary supply of coke for its steel making.

The coalition and Brier Hill Local #1462 both opposed the merger. The coalition wanted any approval of the merger to be conditional upon the sale of the Campbell Works to Community Steel and the guarantee that its products would be bought by the merged corporation. The Brier Hill local asked in addition for the merger to be conditional upon the preservation of the Brier Hill Works. They appeared to have some leverage. The merger would have to be approved by the Justice Department pursuant to a consent decree entered into by LTV when it had purchased Jones & Laughlin. The Anti-Trust Division of the Justice Department did not accept the corporations' argument that Lykes was a failing company that could only be saved by the merger. They recommended against approval.

Power in all of its forms was evident in the companies' next move. They went over the Anti-Trust Division's head to Attorney General Griffin Bell. Despite strong opposition by the assistant attorney general in charge of the Anti-Trust Division, local and district USWA leaders, and the Ecumenical Coalition, Bell eventually approved the merger on June 21, 1978—without conditions. He contended that respectable businessmen would not shade facts and that the Justice Department should think of itself as an ally to businesses trying to help themselves out of trouble.

The role of the myths of legality and the business climate are highlighted in this incident. Those who opposed the merger felt sure that the decision of the Anti-Trust Division would be upheld. It conformed both to the letter of the law and to the conceptions of justice to which the unions, the workers, and the Ecumenical Coalition subscribed. The defeat of their expectations left them stunned and unsure of the next step. The reason given for this decision was a clear statement of the myth of the business climate implying as well that the concerns of the workers and the community were an illegitimate restriction on the interests of business.

The hidden aspects of power and influence may have come merely from the shared beliefs of Attorney General Bell and the corporate officials or from the close professional and social connections between the attorney general and the vice-chairman of the Lykes board of directors. A factor in the decision may have been the two $10,000 contributions of the LTV Political Action Committee to the Democratic National Convention. Whatever the political influences, the decision reflected the lack of political clout of the workers, the unions, and the Ecumenical Coalition.

In the early months of 1978, the coalition concentrated on attaching conditions to the Lykes/LTV merger and beginning the Save Our Valley (SOV) campaign. The campaign was formally inaugurated on February 16 with a rally at a local church accompanied by rousing sermons and gospel singing. The centerpiece of the campaign was the SOV savings account. In order to show local support for Community Steel and to start the community thinking about committing its own resources for a buyout, the coalition arranged for local banks to accept specially designated accounts in which citizens and organizations could deposit savings and be listed as supporters of the Save Our Valley campaign. The depositors' access and use of the money was in no way restricted nor did the coalition have access to the money. While the campaign started slowly, by November of 1978, there were some 4000 SOV accounts containing more than $4,000,000. It was disappointing, however, that the bulk of the money came from local and national church organizations and that few accounts were opened by steel workers themselves.

The Community Steel Project.   In April, preliminary results of the NCEA study were released indicating that the Community Steel project would be feasible and profitable if $300 million in federal loan guarantees could be obtained from the recently established Steel Industry Loan program administered by the EDA. The coalition began to organize seriously on a national basis, opening a New York office, getting commitments from national church organizations, and asking supportive national organizations to put pressure on Washington to aid the Youngstown Project.

The expansion of the coalition's activities accompanied a three-pronged attack on the credibility of the Community Steel project and on the personal and political motivations of the people heading the project. Steel industry executives began their attack by labeling Staughton Lynd and Gar Alperovitz as radicals trying to further a socialist project that could only succeed with massive government aid. Edgar Speer, chairman of U.S. Steel, called the coalition's efforts a "Communist takeover." The Youngstown Chamber of Commerce went as far as to circulate U.S. Labor party pamphlets suggesting that the NCEA was a front organization for infiltrating the Democratic party. Less colorfully, the steel industry and the U.S. Chamber of Commerce took the position that if private steel companies could not make a profit from the closed works, there was no way that a bunch of clerics could do so. This view was regularly communicated to the government agencies considering the Youngstown Project.

Internal government memos also attacked the project and Alperovitz's study. One former EDA official described her boss as being "freaked" by the Alperovitz proposal. The EDA sent several memos to the White House discouraging efforts to commit funds to the Youngstown Project. The EDA counseled against a requested meeting between the coalition and then Vice-President Mondale, arguing that the plan was too radical for the White House to become associated with it, especially before crucial congressional elections. The EDA was concerned as well with protecting its turf in the economic development field. HUD's Urban Development Action Grant (UDAG) program was a recent entry into the field of urban economic development that the EDA saw as its domain. Furthermore, the Steel Industry Loan Fund, which the coalition plan proposed to tap, was made up of repayments of previous EDA loans, and the EDA wished to maintain control of the money. Attempts by HUD, with which Alperovitz had good relations, to rebut criticism of the Youngstown Project were unsuccessful. Because of the elections, however, little word of this controversy reached the coalition until much later.

Jack Watson, a White House aide, told coalition members in Washington that the federal government would commit sufficient funds to the Youngstown Project to assure its success. A final decision on the project was postponed until after the elections. At that point, the White House made it clear that the EDA was to make the decision, and the EDA began to voice its criticisms of the proposal directly to the coalition. The proposal was officially rejected on March 30, 1979, despite numerous revisions having been made to respond to the EDA reservations. Observers intimately acquainted with the process suggest that there was never any intention on the part of the White House to fund the Community Steel project.

Attacks by business and government were not the only ones the Coalition had to face. Up until the very last moment, USWA headquarters echoed the business criticisms. They accused the coalition of being outsiders attempting to foist a radical program on workers and to discredit the union. They too engaged in red-baiting Lynd and Alperovitz. Similar statements by a vice-president of Republic Steel and James Smith, a USWA headquarters staff economist, illustrate how the third face of power operates to block the consideration of alternatives to the traditional political and economic treatment of serious problems. Richard Gray of Republic Steel addressing a Manufacturers' Association meeting warned that "[o]utside interests have been stirring up support amongst the church groups." He called the NCEA an "activist organization" promoting "a socialist adventure, badly conceived." Smith's memo to top USWA officials stated:

> The NCEA paper calls upon our International Union to invest in and promote its plan of community/worker ownership. The writers of the paper are either ignorant of American labor's bad experiences with such schemes [promoted in the nineteenth century by the Knights of Labor], or they know perfectly well what the situation is and are simply seeking to discredit the Union in the eyes of those members who wish to see the Campbell Works reopened. I strongly suspect the latter is the case.

The resistance of USWA headquarters to the Community Steel project was manifested personally by McBride when he and his staff walked out of a meeting during his first visit to Youngstown since the Campbell announcement seven months earlier. The walkout coincided with the introduction of Alperovitz to present the recently completed preliminary feasibility report. Top officials at the 1978 national USWA convention also refused to allow the consideration of a resolution by the Youngstown district locals supporting the efforts to reopen the Campbell Works. Some of McBride's antagonism may have been due to the fact that the Youngstown district gave a majority of its votes to his opponent in the 1977 union election. In any case, after the announcement of the Brier Hill closing in October 1978, James Smith began to work with the coalition. McBride finally endorsed the Community Steel proposal on March 19, 1979, less than two weeks before its rejection by the EDA.

The general inactivity of steel workers themselves can be largely attributed to the workings of the myths of the business climate, big labor, and legality. With their own union leaders and local elites telling them that the coalition efforts were at best foolish and at worst a Communist plot, it is not surprising that they abstained from actively supporting the Community Steel project, especially while they were still receiving substantial unemployment benefits and feared jeopardizing their pensions. Local business elites, echoed by the business press, were also claiming that steel plant closings would prove a boon to the diversified economic development of the region by reducing union power and its effect on local wages.

Only after the unemployment benefits ran out, further closings were announced, workers found themselves still unemployed or underemployed, and the USWA began to support efforts to reopen the closed plants did workers step to the fore of the movement. By then, it was too late. The federal government had already refused aid, an extremely conservative administration was in power, the steel companies had girded themselves for opposition, and many of the workers had already taken other employment and left the region. Earlier, more aggressive, worker-initiated action might have had an effect. This is indicated by information obtained by the coalition that the initial angry reaction of workers along with pubic opinion about the Campbell closing had postponed the closing of the U.S. Steel Youngstown Works by almost two years. Notices to U.S. Steel workers had been in the envelopes when the Campbell announcement was made. U.S. Steel then hired Superintendent Kirwan to try and save the Youngstown Works and to prepare for the reaction if the closing was deemed necessary.

Table 4–1 shows the chronology of major actions initiated by Youngstown workers. It serves to highlight the contrast between worker participation at Youngstown and at Longwy.

Longwy

Despite the similar goal of preserving steel industry jobs in the region, the actors, tactics, and goals of the Longwy struggle were generally very different from those at Youngstown. The ultimate goal at Longwy was not merely to prevent the closing of certain steel mills or to reopen them, but to develop a coordinated industrial plan under which the steel industry could grow both in the Lorraine and nationally. Longwy workers thought not only in terms of preserving their own jobs but also in terms of assuring steel industry employment to their children. The workers themselves were the major actors at Longwy both through their inter-union committee that initiated most of the local actions and through their national trade union federations that channeled support to the locals and maintained national political pressure. The tactics of the Longwy workers, as already indicated above, were decidedly different from those of the Youngstown actors— although in both cases, they led up to negotiations with the government and with the steel corporations and ultimately failed in achieving the intended goals. The contrast is most evident when considering the actions at Longwy in the first three months of 1979 during which time the negotiations began.

Immediately following the closing announcements of December 11 and 12, 1979, several days of locally oriented action began with the CFDT Metalworkers Union publication of an economic development plan for the Lorraine called the "The Future of the Steel Industry." The plan proposed that steel industry jobs would be preserved by increasing steel production and by better linking steel production with upstream and downstream industries. At the same time, the Fédération Générale de Métallurgie-Confédération Française Democratique du Travail (FGM-

Table 4-1   Chronology of Youngstown Worker Action

1977

Sept. 19–22   Workers gather over 100,000 signatures for a petition addressed to the government demanding aid and protection for the steel industry.

Sept. 23   250 workers deliver the petition to Capitol Hill after failing to see the President.

Oct. 14   Militant unionist, Gerald Dickey, secretary of Brier Hill Local #1462, and ad hoc union group threaten shareholders suit against Youngstown Sheet & Tube. (Suit later barred by USWA District Director Leseganich on instructions from USWA headquarters.)

1978

Jan. 23   Local and district union leaders meet with Department of Justice to protest Lykes/LTV merger.

June 30   Local union leaders request meeting with Lykes/LTV to discuss future of Brier Hill Works.

Sept. 16   Local unionists and coalition members picket speech of President Carter in Columbus. Carter avoids pickets by change of itinerary.

Dec. 14   Local and district union leaders meet with Jones & Laughlin (owned by Lykes/LTV) management and are told there is no hope for saving Brier Hill.

Dec. 15   Meeting of Youngstown steel locals decides to send letters of protest to Lykes/LTV and to picket Brier Hill.

Dec. 29   200 unionists picket Brier Hill.

1979

Jan. 19   Meeting with Lykes/LTV, national and local union leaders. Local unionists' intention to invite local and national politicians and coalition members nixed by both company and USWA headquarters.

Jan. 22   Local #1462 members picket and confront superintendent of Youngstown Sheet & Tube at country club.

Mar. 12   Steelworkers United for Employment (SUE), an organization of unemployed steel workers, is formed and approves labor plan for Community Steel at a public meeting.

Mar. 17   Downtown rally planned by Local #1462 flops. Only about 250 attend.

Mar. 30   Local unions agree with company on orderly shutdown of Brier Hill.

Table 4-1   Chronology of Youngstown Worker Action *(continued)*

Apr. 10	Rank and file vote to approve orderly shutdown agreement by 2–1 margin in light turnout.
July 11	Local unions and environmental groups agree on lawsuit against Army Corps of Engineers permission for U.S. Steel to construct a new steel plant in Conneaut, Ohio.
Nov. 28	Local unionists tell old coalition members that workers will lead fight against U.S. Steel closings.
Nov. 29	Steel workers meet to plan picketing. USWA District Director Leseganich says he will not participate.
Nov. 30	Demonstration and occupation of U.S. Steel Pittsburgh headquarters by 1000 steel workers.
Dec. 21	Lawsuit filed against U.S. Steel by local unions and U.S. Representative Williams.
1980	
Jan. 28	Rally and occupation of Youngstown offices of U.S. Steel by 300 workers.
Feb. 12	Local union group offers to buy U.S. Steel Ohio and McDonald Works for $20 million. U.S. Steel refuses to sell to "government aided competitor." Refusal added to antitrust claim of lawsuit.
July 25	Appeal of judgment allowing U.S. Steel to close and dismantle Youngstown Works loses. Antitrust claim goes to trial.
Nov. 15	Antitrust claim settled by promise of U.S. Steel to keep mills intact for five years for lease or purchase by worker group or other private parties.
1981	
Aug. 25	Steel loan guarantee fund abolished by Reagan administration. Community Steel project dropped despite offer of money for feasibility study.

CFDT) recognized the need for new industries in the Lorraine to assure future employment for the region's youth. The midpoint of this crucial three-month period in 1979 was also marked by a nationally oriented event—an industry-wide, 24-hour strike. The period closed with the march on Paris by 120,000 steel workers and their supporters.

Amidst and between these landmark events came the opening of separate negotiations with the government and the steel companies. This period was also punctuated by an increase in militancy, large local demonstrations, and stepped-up "strike force" tactics. The interunion committee organized a demonstration of 45,000 at Metz with the assistance of the left-wing political parties and several merchants' groups. On January 24, 12,000 schoolchildren demonstrated at Longwy. The following day, the teachers' union struck and students and teachers demonstrated. On February 16, the national day of action, 80,000 demonstrated at Metz while Longwy merchants closed their shops, declaring Longwy a ghost town (*ville morte*). Women's groups organized a women's demonstration in Longwy–Bas, and on March 10, 35,000 people demonstrated in Denain.

The increasing militancy was manifest in the large number of occupations, blockades, and even bombings and sackings during the period. Twice, police intervention was met by attacks on the local police headquarters. A bloody confrontation was avoided in the second instance only by the redirection of the workers' hostility to the Metallurgical Employers' Association chambers, which were sacked and burned. Bombings occurred at the offices of the local employment service, the tax collector, and the temporary workers agency. The office of Usinor's chief of personnel was first occupied and then moved out into the street. In addition to the occupation of steel company offices and meeting rooms, banks and communication centers were special targets. Confrontations with the police occurred during the occupation of the local television relay station. At one point, this relay was used to broadcast the workers' own program "SOS Emploi." The CFDT and the CGT created their own radio stations and began broadcasts. The powerful CGT station, *Lorraine Coeur d'Acier* (Lorraine Heart of Steel), became the beacon of the struggle generating great popular support.

Work stoppages were frequent during this period. Several times, raw materials and energy supplies to the mills were cut off. Several of the occupations and "strike force" operations took place in Paris, coordinated by the national trade union federations. Just prior to the massive Paris demonstration on March 23, metro stations were occupied and toll booths were seized— "liberating" the tolls and fares for the support of the struggle.

Banners were unfurled on the towers of Notre Dame, and the Eiffel Tower was occupied.

This period also represents the height of the organizational activities; that is, the creation of a movement. Longwy workers sent delegations to other steel communities, many of which were less affected by the announced layoffs, asking for their support in the struggle. In general, these requests were well received but only in direct proportion to the extent a community foresaw itself affected by the contraction of the steel industry. Although not as frequent as in the Longwy area itself, work stoppages and demonstrations were widespread. Steel workers from these other towns helped to swell the numbers of the march on Paris.

Negotiations between the trade unions and the government began in Paris on February 6, 1979. The unions demanded to discuss the overall industrial plan that they deemed inadequate. Minister of Labor Boulin maintained the position that the government could only discuss the plans for benefits and methods of workforce reduction. With this impasse continuing and worker militancy rising, on February 28, Minister of Industry Giraud unilaterally announced the formation of "reconversion firms" in which displaced workers would work and receive training until other jobs were found for them. This strategy was partially successful. The FO, the most conservative and smallest of the three major trade union federations, dropped out of the interunion committee and agreed to accept the industrial plan as a given. The CGT and CFDT maintained their call for negotiations first on the restructuring itself. The CGT presented the government with a nationwide petition calling for a revitalized and expanded steel industry. The government then turned the next stage of negotiations over to the steel companies.

On March 6, four months of negotiations between the unions and the directors of Sacilor–Sollac and Usinor began. The directors also maintained that the industry plan was irrevocable, pointing to the government and EEC policies. While these meetings were going on, the minister of labor announced (again unilaterally) an increase in the benefits for the displaced, including 50,000-franc bonuses (about $10,000 at the time) for "voluntary" departures and early retirement at age 50. He further guaranteed that no layoffs would take place during the negotiations. (This guarantee was later rescinded.) Clearly, the tough tactics of the unions were having their effect.

Immediately following the march on Paris, several concessions were made by the government and the steel industry. On March 27, Usinor agreed to discuss the timing and necessity of the closing of Usinor–Longwy. The minister of labor announced voluntary departure bonuses of 60,000 francs for immigrant workers and a policy of job creation in the Lorraine—promising more than 7000 new industrial jobs before the end of 1983. On May 17, all of the unions except the CGT and the Longwy metal workers local of the CFDT agreed to negotiate with the Metallurgical Employers' Association. The CGT, while refraining from participation, attended the negotiations. These negotiations continued for two months. At the same time, there was a noticeable decrease in worker militancy, partly in expectation of favorable negotiations but mostly in preparation for the financial and psychological hardships of the now inevitable job loss. Despite this seeming spirit of resignation, a referendum held by Longwy-area mayors in October 1979 indicated that 98% of the voters still supported the building of another steel mill in Longwy, as had been promised in 1964.

On July 24, 1979, the Paris negotiations ended with the signing of an accord providing substantial social benefits and a policy of job reduction *en douceur.* The restructuring would be achieved without layoffs. Of the more than 21,000 job reductions in the steel industry nationally, 12,500 would be accounted for by early retirements, 4800 workers would choose the voluntary departure bonuses, and 4000 would be transferred to other facilities. Longwy workers were promised transfers to other plants in the Lorraine (a promise that was later broken in several cases). The only concession on the industrial plan itself was made by Usinor, which postponed 2300 of its projected job reductions nationally— about 600 of those postponements affected Longwy workers.

A Comparative Analysis of the Events

Different Responses to an Agenda Set Elsewhere

Youngstown and Longwy provide excellent illustrations of how power that is out of the reach of public scrutiny and debate can be used to fix the agenda as well as the arena of struggle. The failure of the efforts to preserve steel industry jobs in both towns is

testimony to the overwhelming power of capital even where
workers rejected the myths that gave the power its legitimacy.
This ultimate similarity will be discussed more fully in the con-
cluding chapter. This chapter will conclude with an analysis of the
different actors, tactics, goals, and intermediate results of the two
struggles in terms of the role and acceptance or rejection of the
myths of big labor, the business climate, and legality.

Kourchid has suggested that in both situations the companies
and the government worked together to fix the agenda to which
the workers and their supporters had to respond. In the process,
they delayed decisions and camouflaged decision makers until
worker resistance had attenuated, and they individualized and
divided workers by using bonuses, benefits, and pensions in order
to demobilize workers.[16] While these tactics were effective at
both Youngstown and Longwy in preventing major changes in the
extent of workforce reduction, they were not equally effective.

At Youngstown, from the outset, the tactics prevented widespread worker militancy in challenging the layoffs and closings.
This was certainly not the case at Longwy. There, despite the
efforts at concealing the decisionmakers and despite substantial
concessions in the form of benefits and a policy of *douceur,* the
restructuring of the steel industry was ultimately viewed as a
naked exercise of the economic and political power of capital
(through a captive government). This substantially discredited
the Giscard–Barre government, leading to their ouster in May of
1981 and the nationalization of several large companies. In other
words, the government and business failed in their efforts to
clothe the use of economic and political power in myth and to
make the closings and economic dislocation seem legitimate and
inevitable to the public and to the workers themselves. In the end,
the workers at Longwy won more concessions than those at
Youngstown; however, recent events in France have demonstrated the great resilience and reserve strength of capital.

Institutional Supports for Worker Militancy

The forms and militancy of labor struggles depend on institutional supports and belief systems. The greater militancy of the
Longwy workers stems in part from the stronger institutional
support these efforts received in three key areas.

The first important area of support, which differed distinctly from the Youngstown case, was the full and early involvement of the national trade union federations. In contrast to the reaction of the United Steel Workers headquarters, French trade union leaders spoke out early and often in support of the workers' efforts to preserve steel industry jobs. They provided financial support, a national forum, research services, an alternative plan, and access to the top corporate and governmental levels. The leadership of both the CGT and CFDT had developed detailed proposals for preserving steel jobs and modernizing the industry even before the closing announcements. These served as points of support for mobilizing worker opposition to the government and corporate plan.

Immediately following the announcements, the leadership of the major federation denounced the planned restructuring as ill-conceived and developed without any worker consultation. National leaders of the CGT and CFDT appeared in Longwy soon after the announcements to show personal support for the workers' efforts. Henry Krasucki, second in command and soon to be head of the CGT, associated himself intimately with worker militancy by meeting striking workers inside the occupied Longwy–Usinor plant and highly praising their resistance. The mutual support of the local workers and the national federations continued until all but the CGT agreed to negotiate benefits and workforce reduction methods. While some of the Longwy workers, most notably those of the CFDT, felt sold out by that agreement, most recognized the difficulty of the negotiators' position. The CFDT and CGT leadership fully recognized the important effects of worker militancy and, indeed, the willingness to act illegally on the progress of the negotiations and the concessions ultimately received.

The second area of institutional support that differed greatly between Youngstown and Longwy involved elected officials and political parties. In Youngstown as in the United States generally, neither major political party supported labor militancy. The general concern of Youngstown-area politicians, whether Democratic or Republican, was economic development, not necessarily preserving steel industry jobs. This oriented political efforts in two directions: toward the federal government for funding and toward attracting outside investment. Militant labor actions were regarded as detrimental to both of these endeavors. The specific concern of Youngstown-area politicians was who would control the economic development funding when it arrived. This caused a great deal of political in-fighting and fragmented support for any specific development plan. The ambiguity of political positions was exemplified by Congressman Charles Carney, a Youngstown Democrat. He was instrumental in the creation of the Mahoning Valley Economic Development Commission (MVEDC) to receive EDA funds. The MVEDC became a rival to the already established Western Reserve Economic Development Agency (WREDA). With Carney's support and with a Democratic administration in power, the MVEDC was able to take federal contracts and funds from the older agency.

The MVEDC also had close ties with the Youngstown Chamber of Commerce, which tended to see the steel closings and layoffs as something of a blessing, if a mixed one. The chamber was eager to bring new businesses into the area which they believed would be facilitated by breaking the hold of the high-wage, unionized steel industry on the local labor market. While Carney eventually supported the Ecumenical Coalition's efforts to set up Community Steel, his support was never more than lukewarm. In any case, he was defeated in the 1978 election and replaced by Republican Congressman Lyle Williams. WREDA, on the other hand, was supportive of the idea of reopening the Campbell Works, and it provided the initial favorable feasibility study. WREDA Executive Director Sullivan, a Republican, considered the coalition's Community Steel proposal too radical. Sullivan favored the reopening of Campbell on a phased-in basis by a private, but locally managed, firm.[17] Because he had done much high quality contract work on the Youngstown steel industry for the EDA and the Commerce Department, these agencies listened to Sullivan despite their political obligations to Carney and the MVEDC.

Nationally, as well as locally, neither worker militancy nor a worker/community buyout were seen as legitimate responses to the problems of the steel industry. The Democratic administration had already begun a policy of austerity aimed at cutting inflation and the federal deficit at the expense of employment and aid to the unemployed. Aside from Senators Edward M. Kennedy (D–Mass.) and Howard M. Metzenbaum (D–Ohio) and some members of the Congressional Steel Caucus, little national support was accorded to the coalition's proposal or to pressuring the steel companies to preserve employment in Youngstown. National, primarily Democratic party, efforts were directed at temporary funds for dealing with unemployment and attempts to give some of what the steel industry and the USWA had jointly asked for in terms of relaxed pollution control regulations and import quotas, along with encouraging steel plant moderniza-tions.

By contrast, worker militancy at Longwy found immediate political support at both the local and national levels. Three-quarters of the Longwy-area population lived under left-wing, mostly Communist, mayors. The mayors and their parties helped to organize, as well as participated in, several of the demonstra-tions. Local town halls were important communication centers for the struggle. Radio Lorraine Cour d'Acier was established in the town hall of Longwy–Haut. Nationally, the Communist and Socialist parties took up the workers' cause in condemning the government's plan for restructuring the steel industry. Their shared critique of the government and their agreement on the need for the nationalization of the steel industry allowed them to reestablish the union of the left that had broken down in the 1978 elections.

This steel industry was an important issue in the Socialist vic-tory of 1981, with the above-noted ironic results. Preparation for the upcoming elections, in which steel industry policy would be an important issue, encouraged worker mobilization in Longwy. Many workers who doubted the achievement of immediately favorable results saw the struggle as a prelude to the legislative and presidential elections of 1981. They saw themselves as work-ing for *"le changement."* As one worker declared, "Political change is necessary: there's nothing else for it. So long as we have Giscard and Barre, we're going backwards."[18] Most importantly, this political support gave the workers national spokespersons who could mobilize public opinion for their cause.

The third difference in institutional support is in the extent that the community closed ranks behind the steel workers; that is, the extent of community solidarity. Here too, Longwy steel workers clearly had much greater support than those at Youngstown. Demonstrations were well attended by local citizens; merchants not only participated in actions called by the interunion committee but formed their own support group; and school teachers were at the forefront of the mobilization efforts.[19] One reason for this is that Longwy and its environs were considerably more mono-industrial than Youngstown. More than half of local employment depended directly on the steel industry in Longwy, less than a third at Youngstown. Little manufacturing employment existed outside of the steel industry at Longwy, whereas the Youngstown area possessed automobile and rubber industry facilities. Another important reason is that the same belief systems (particularly the myths of the business climate and big labor) that stifled worker resistance to the shutdown at Youngstown operated with equal force among the citizens. Many citizens, while expressing sympathy for laid-off workers, suggested that the workers and their unions had brought the trouble on themselves by their excessive power. Small business owners, often hurt indirectly by the steel closings, opined that these closings would allow small business to flourish in the valley. A persistent theme was that workers, unions, the government, and clergy should not intrude in business decisions—this was the domain of owners and managers. Workers and trade unions generally regarded themselves as unqualified to make such decisions.[20]

Belief Systems and Worker Militancy

Worker and community solidarity in Longwy was significantly greater than that in Youngstown, in part because French workers attached greater importance to their jobs. As mentioned in Chapter 3, the French ideal of a job stresses the integration of worklife and social life. Comparative data indicate that American workers tend more toward a view of employment that stresses its role as a means to leisure time activities and a social life distinct from work associations.

In a comparative study of French and American workers' attitudes in the midst of economic crisis, Olivier Kourchid found significant differences that contribute to worker solidarity and militancy. American workers tended to place "economic liberty" and "mobility" high on their scale of important values. In contrast, French workers place "quality of life" much higher. Most American workers thought competition "allows the best to rise," while French workers overwhelmingly saw competition as divisive. American workers saw their work as primarily providing an income that enables them to have "other projects" for the future.

French workers regarded secure employment as a value in itself.

French workers, despite a similarly low rate of union membership, had a much higher regard for trade unions. They, much more often than their American counterparts, expected trade unions to act toward and succeed in preserving jobs. Most importantly, two-thirds of the French workers surveyed saw collective action as being able to protect jobs—less than one-third of the Americans surveyed believed this. It is not surprising, then, that French workers saw solidarity as growing during economic crisis while American workers saw it as declining—despite the fact that the vast majority of both groups felt that greater solidarity was the appropriate response of workers to economic crisis.

Even more clear evidence of the workings of the third face of power was the finding regarding economic layoffs, transfers, and shorter hours. Such measures were considered to be "certain" results of the economic crisis by 10–15% of the French and only 1–6% of the American respondents, whereas 30–40% of the Americans and only 12-13% of the French considered them "impossible." These results suggest how power and myth work in a hidden but potent way. Kourchid concludes:[21]

> *In any case, one can only ask oneself once more about that capacity of American firms to persuade their employees that they have such job security when they have, in fact, a much greater chance of being laid-off or transferred than their French counterparts.*

One of the more militant trade unionists at Youngstown explicitly acknowledged the power of the business myth among steel workers and in the community. In his efforts to convince others to actively support a worker/community buyout, he frequently made the following speech:[22]

> *There [are] certain examples out there. A guy like Onassis. He went to Argentina with two hundred bucks, and ends up owning all the ships in Greece. He never limited himself in what he thought he could do. . . . [A] hundred million dollars wouldn't bother Onassis, would it? Just like Onassis. We'll get it. It's there. Keep going.*

Another important difference in the institutions and belief systems that influenced worker actions is the history of recent social movements in the two countries. The efforts to preserve steel jobs at Youngstown and Longwy borrowed forms of action from recent social movements. At Youngstown, the formation of the Ecumenical Coalition and the efforts to achieve community controlled economic development through massive federal financial aid were a repeat of organizational modes common during the War on Poverty of the late sixties. As in the sixties, the activities at Youngstown involved Legal Services Program attorneys (one of whom was Staughton Lynd) and legal action and negotiations. The worker-led movement against U.S. Steel held sit-ins and demonstrations reminiscent of the civil rights and antiwar movements, along with the continuation of litigation.

These echoes of the recent past should not be condemned as foolish. They had, in their time, created new centers of power in American society and had temporarily created confidence in a better future for groups that had seen themselves as oppressed and powerless. It is important to note, however, that a major characteristic of these efforts was their initiation and leadership by community elites.

The forms of action undertaken in Longwy reflected the quasi-insurrectional tactics of May–June 1968 and the factory occupation movement spawned by the LIP Watch Co. strike and occupation. These events had given rise to a spurt of confidence in new forms of worker power. The hot summer of 1968 resulted in the Grenelle Protocol that gave workers the right to organize at the plant level. The LIP action generated much public support for workers taking charge of their own workplaces in order to protect their jobs. These events were also convincing arguments for the power of solidarity among workers and between workers and other groups, even against the forces of capital and of order.

The Politics of Youngstown: Power and Pluralism

The Assumptions of Pluralism

Kourchid suggests that the different belief systems of American and French workers, as manifested in the contrasting actions at Youngstown and Longwy, can be characterized as "economic" and "political" respectively.[23] On the surface, this distinction seems reasonable in that the Youngstown efforts were directed at reopening the closed plants on a private, commercial basis by finding new, local sources of capital, and at Longwy the major point of the struggle was the reorientation of the national steel industry policy. Behind this surface distinction, however, are profound political differences.

The movement of the Ecumenical Coalition to the forefront of the job preservation efforts and the relatively minor role of the

USWA reflect important and recurrent features of the American political process. The fragmentation and competition of local political actors leading to the inability to produce any unified or effective response to the closings are characteristic of that process. The organizing, public opinion mobilization, and negotiation efforts directed at obtaining federal financial support for the Community Steel project are also characteristic. The opposing belief systems that contributed greatly to the differing forms of struggle at Youngstown and Longwy are best characterized as divergent conceptions of *politics*—one, often called "pluralist," based on the supposition of a rule-governed consensus underlying a competitive political process and the other based on the supposition of unresolved social conflict more or less hidden or suppressed by a formal and deceptive political process.[24]

The pluralist conception that is prevalent in the analysis of American politics, including labor politics, assumes a society in which the resources for influencing important political decisions are distributed unequally among members of the society, but not cumulatively so. To elaborate, these resources include money, organizational strength capable of mobilizing a significant number of people, political skill and knowledge, the time and intensity of interest for engaging in politics, and the capacity to influence public opinion. The distribution of these resources in society is unequal in the sense that each individual or group possesses more or less of these resources than others. Pluralist theory maintains that despite the unequal distribution, the resources are widely distributed such that no individual or group can dominate (or accumulate) all or most important public decisions. With this notion guiding their decision, the USWA local at the Ohio Works opened a Save Our Valley account. The local's president stated:[25]

> At the Ohio Works of US Steel, we are operating under many of the same conditions that workers at the Campbell Works experienced before that plant closed. Our deposit of $10,000 is an effort to say to the nation that we're willing to help ourselves restore steel jobs and protect existing ones.

A second element of the American conception of politics is that the principal actors in the political system are groups of two types. The first consists of relatively stable associations, such as ethnic, professional, and religious groups, that have an array of interests with different priorities linked to the protection and development of the group, the diffusion of the group's values in the society at

large, and the well-being of the group's members. The second
type of group is organized around a single issue and is generally
less stable. Its membership fluctuates according to the importance of the group's issue in public opinion and public debate.

The groups follow their interests, in theory defined or at least
embraced by the members, using their accumulated resources. A
group's resources are seen as an important measure of its potential
influence. Thus, the Save Our Valley accounts were created to
"enable advocates of the new steel operation to show, in solid
figures, how much support they can expect from the community."[26] The manager of the campaign for the Ecumenical Coalition told how another of their key resources, press coverage, was
to be used:[27]

> *We were on a very fast track, and we sensed that we could manipulate
> the federal government through the press, and convince the federal
> government through the press that the whole community was behind
> us. I think that the federal government, at one point, sensed that there
> was a strong local, regional, and national reaction to this closing and
> that they'd better do something.*

The resources are limited by the fact that people do not belong
to only one group, but to several often representing incompatible
interests. This was one of the keenly felt restraints on the religious
leaders in the Ecumenical Coalition. Their congregations included people from labor and management and from the small
business community; that is, people on both sides of the Community Steel controversy. The USWA also suffered from this problem. Different locals in the Youngstown district were affected
differently by the shutdowns, giving rise to divergent views on
how to deal with them. As James Smith noted:[28]

> *Part of our whole problem in Youngstown was the fact that our
> members were somewhat fragmented into the different locals. If we
> had one local union in the whole complex with one elected set of
> leadership, we would have been able to do more than we did.*

A third aspect of the pluralist conception of politics is its
assumption of a widespread consensus on the "rules of the game"
and a notion of "fair play." These are closely related to the myth of
legality. They require that hard political work by legitimate organized groups be rewarded by some influence over the decisions
and issues important to them. Lloyd McBride gave voice to these

expectations when he finally supported the coalition's efforts in a letter to President Carter:[29]

> *Under the leadership of the churches of that area, and the religious community network through the United States, a new spirit of community determination has been forged in the midst of the Youngstown tragedy. Labor, management, and public officials are working together more closely than ever before. They are convinced that by hard work and close cooperation they can rebuild the economic base of their community. To do so they need the sort of basic financial support which only the Federal Government can provide.*

In analyzing the failure of the Community Steel project, Bob Vasquez, president of Local #1330 at the Ohio Works, told Staughton Lynd that one of the fundamental errors he and other unionists had made was to accept these assumptions and expect fairness in the negotiations with U.S. Steel and the federal government. He extended this observation to his expectations from the federal courts.[30]

Pluralism Reinforced by the Courts

The courts are, indeed, important institutions for raising to mythic status the pluralist notion that there are underlying, shared rules in American politics, including labor politics. U.S. District Judge Thomas D. Lambros, who presided over the case challenging the closing of U.S. Steel's Youngstown Works, often stated his understanding of these rules. His first concern was the primacy of the "free enterprise system" and that government intrusion in it "could upset the very foundation upon which our country is built." Noting, however, that "we deal with human relationships," the judge found another underlying rule to be that "we try to deal with those human relationships so as to maintain stability and control those human relationships in a manner to maintain stability and tranquility."

Having established and generalized to all social relationships, the primacy of the myth of the business climate, the judge then gave support to an underlying notion of fairness as well as to the myth of legality. He hinted that the "lengthy, long-established relationship between United States Steel, the steel industry as an institution, the community in Youngstown, the people in Mahoning County and the Mahoning Valley in having given and devoted their lives to this industry" gives rise to a "property right to the extent that U.S. Steel cannot leave that Mahoning Valley and the Youngstown area in a state of waste, that it cannot completely abandon its obligation to that community, because certain vested rights have arisen out of this long relationship and institution." In the end, he decided to the contrary, referring the Youngstown steel workers to the legislative and collective bargaining processes with the pluralist reminder that with their resources, "labor unions, now more aware of the importance of this problem, will begin to bargain for relocation adjustment funds and mechanisms."[31] He had found the answer to a pressing political–legal problem in the myth of big labor.

The assumption of an underlying consensus on the rules of the political game emphasizes, as Judge Lambros suggested, the importance of the maintenance of stability, tranquility, and order. It is assumed that each group is able, without violence or the rejection of legality, to have its interests considered in public decisions according to its resources, the number of its supporters, and the intensity of their support for the group's interests. So it was that Bishop Malone and the Presbyterian leaders withdrew from the coalition after the the EDA rejected the loan fund application. They cited their inability to accept street demonstrations and occupations as legitimate tactics.

Weighing Group Influence

Under the pluralist resource calculus, citizens are able to have their most important interests addressed in public policy through the groups to which they belong. Some groups, however, appear to be excluded from this process. Kay Schlozman and Sidney Verba maintain that such is the case for the unemployed who according to all of their investigations "are not an active force. They are, in the words of one government official, 'a political zero.'" This condition persists until massive and chronic unemployment disturbs public order and tranquility.[32]

The characteristic mode of political action in a pluralist system is interest aggregation by bargaining, compromise, and the exchange of services and support among the groups. The government functions as an arena where the groups jockey for position. A graphic example of this was the filing of a large number of *amicus curiae* (friend of the court) briefs by interest groups on both sides of the controversy in the attempt to influence the federal court's decision *(Local 1330, USWA* v. *U.S. Steel)*. The government also functions as a referee to resolve disputes on the rules of the game and, in the end, as the scale on which the influence of each group is weighed. The interests of each group are taken account of proportionately in the resulting decision.

During the course of the coalition's activities to preserve steel jobs in Youngstown, its influence and that of its allies fluctuated greatly on the government's scale. In an early visit to Youngstown, HUD Secretary, Patricia Harris, declared:[33]

> *This commendable community support is precisely the sort of effort we are looking for in developing new Federal strategies to support areas like Youngstown that are determined to help themselves when faced with devastating plant closings.*

Later, the EDA's evaluation of the influence of the coalition and its consultant, the National Center for Economic Alternatives, was decidedly less positive compared to that of other groups interested in the outcome of the government's decision. A briefing memo from the EDA to the White House prior to the coalition's September 27, 1978, meeting with presidential aide Jack Watson indicates that the political decision to reject the Community Steel project was based as much or more on the relative influence of the groups than on the substance of their proposals:[34]

> *NCEA is less important than the other organizations [USWA, WREDA, MVEDC] mentioned. It will recommend the unfeasible solution of spending vast sums of Federal dollars to reopen a facility which will never regain its market share let alone be self-sustaining. Moreover, NCEA and its ideas are strongly opposed by the Steel Workers Union and by private industry.*

The community groups mentioned above, however, played the competitive pluralist game to such an extent that they could neither agree on a response to the closings nor allow the other groups to proceed independently. This situation was highlighted in a "Business Beat" column in the *Youngstown Vindicator*:[35]

> *If the member communities of CASTLO—an acronym for Camp-bell, Struthers, and Lowellville—aren't celebrating their share of a likely grant to the Mahoning Valley Economic Development Com-mittee, it's because they feel they're being used.*
>
> *CASTLO project director George Wilson huddled with state Sen. Harry Meshel, D–33, last week over whether the group should accept*

$60,000 of a $600,000 U.S. Economic Development Administration grant to MVEDC. Wilson believes MVEDC is capitalizing on the economic plight of the three cities that were hardhit by last year's layoffs at Youngstown Sheet and Tube. His feeling is that the impact of the layoffs are centered in the CASTLO cities, but federal assistance may be distributed throughout the two-county region.

"We've got some problems with the MVEDC's community development strategy," Wilson acknowledged. "We believe the effort should be directed at us."

This political fragmentation soon produced a stalemate and a justification for the refusal of further federal aid. Pluralist politics often results in stalemate; however, stalemate and inaction are not neutral. They generally work to the advantage of those private groups and organizations that already have great economic resources and power.

The coalition's telegram responding to the rejection of their application for EDA loan guarantees indicated that they felt they had played the game of pluralist politics and that they expected the rules of the game and the weighing of influence to result in a different decision. The telegram read:[36]

We believe that the March 29 letter reflects a collapse of the pre-1978 election assurances passed out by you on behalf of President Carter to the unemployed of the Mahoning Valley....

The enormous efforts by the religious denominations, including the U.S. Catholic Conference, the National Council of Churches, the Synagogue Council of America, were undertaken in faithful reliance on the good will and concern of the federal government and, during the past six months, on your own assurances of last fall.

We believe now, in the light of the March 29 letter, that we were misdirected in our efforts and our reliance.

Labor politics inside the unions is guided by the pluralist assumptions. Because the legal existence of the union at the local level depends on the constant support or at least acquiescence by a majority of the workers inside a plant, far-reaching or radical political demands and even opinions are suppressed in the search for the lowest common denominator of shared interests. At the national level, legitimation in the pluralist game of interest aggregation again requires rejecting radical stances and illegal tactics while cultivating alliances with groups whose overall support for the labor movement and the real interests of workers is nil.

In a letter to the editor of the *Brier Hill Unionist,* Ken Doran, a Brier Hill worker, commented on the role of the USWA's pluralist politics in the failure to preserve basic steel jobs:[37]

> *The United Steel Workers of America, a major labor union possessing a power base from which they could influence corporate decisions on plant shutdowns and the modernization of the steel industry, has remained virtually silent.*
>
> *I think over the years many factors have led to this position by the USWA. Its development as a narrow-interest trade union association instead of a class-conscious labor organization was one factor. Union acceptance of corporate capitalism at home and allegiance to corporate economic expansion overseas are other factors.*
>
> *The union's independence and integrity have been sacrificed to corporate policies that have provoked wars and the associated negative aspects of such wars. In the process the steelworkers union has assisted in the creation of multinational corporations which now threaten the economic and psychological security of the very workers the Union should protect.*

Group Legitimation

It is evident why American pluralist politics can be taken for an economic conception—it shares much with neoclassical economic theory. Pluralist politics assumes a veritable political market with free exchanges of resources, where the interplay of narrow interests (governed by a neutral and unseen hand) results in the allocation of political influence. Pluralism, democracy, and capitalism are often intentionally confounded by political actors. It helps to perpetuate the myth that democracy, defined by American pluralist politics, is inseparable from a capitalist market economy. For example, Father Ed Stanton, the coalition staff director had to convince the public, and particularly the business community, that the Community Steel project and the efforts to promote it were not "creeping socialism," but "the best of capitalism: a lot of people putting their money and labor together.... It's pure capitalism."[38]

Moreover, neoclassical economic theory is hidden behind the pluralist notion of "interest" as the maximization of resources or of political and economic power. The pluralist "rules of the game" discourage the pursuit of major social and economic changes that would require the reevaluation of "interest" as a political notion.[39]

This narrow notion of interest was an important obstacle to the Ecumenical Coalition's total embrace of pluralist politics. Their reservations in accepting such a narrow, economically oriented conception may well have contributed to the disdain for their competence and the suspicion with which their efforts were met—and ultimately to their failure. The Thanksgiving pastoral letter of November 1977 shows that while they ultimately embraced the pluralist conception, they had to wrestle with the legitimation of their group and its interest in this politico-economic issue.

The letter begins with the attempt to legitimate the interest of clerics in decisions about economic development and the fate of the steel industry.[40] It emphasizes traditional interests of the clergy, "the human and community consequences of [the economic] losses—the strains on marriage and family life, increased depression, alcoholism and alienation." It goes on to note that:

> [t]his closing has already contributed to greater distrust and antagonism between various elements in our community. Behind the statistics and headlines lie individuals, families and communities left vulnerable and fearful by this decision. This is not in any sense a purely economic problem.

Group legitimation also requires that a group have resources that can be brought to bear in advancing its interests. If the group wishes to be courted by other groups in the process of interest aggregation, it may present its resources as special in some way. The letter accomplishes this in two ways. First, it suggests the special role of the clergy as teachers with access to large numbers of people. Words such as "teaching" and "education" and phrases of similar import occur often in the text. The Scriptures are referred to as "a rich resource in dealing with issues of economic and social life." Second, it specifies an initial commitment to give time and funds (with a reminder of the churches' already substantial role in social service delivery) to plans for aiding the unemployed, including the study of alternatives to a permanent shutdown.

The letter also declares the coalition's understanding and acceptance of the rules of the game. It specifies the role of the coalition as one interest among many and its acceptance of the need for alliance formation, negotiation, and compromise in the competition to influence public decisions:

It is our intention to provide a common ground and an impetus for community efforts without substituting for other legitimate interests. We do not wish to take the place of leaders in the industry, union leaders, business representatives and government officials. Rather, we seek to avoid political rivalry and organizational conflict. Motivated by pastoral concern we wish to raise issues, serve our community and call upon these and other groups to play their essential roles in restoring and rebuilding the economic vitality of our Valley.

We wish to cooperate with other groups and individuals seeking remedies to this crisis. We are eager to join our efforts to those of the workers and their unions, political officials, responsible business and corporate leaders, and other members of the Mahoning Valley seeking to restore the economic health of our community.

... We will also attempt to help national leaders and organizations understand the dimensions of our crisis . . . .

We call upon the members of our community to join together in a comprehensive plan of action to develop the will, the resources and the commitment to revitalize the Valley. This effort will require the cooperation of every sector of Youngstown: churches, synagogues, labor, business, financial institutions, government, and other organizations and individuals.

The expectations of fairness, reward for economic and political hard work, respect for legality, and the belief in the legitimacy and ultimate reconcilability of competing interests under established rules, certainly limited and possibly misdirected the responses of workers and clergy in Youngstown. Few actors in Youngstown, contrary to the prevailing view in Longwy, viewed the relationship of the government and the steel industry as one of collusion in preventing worker and community participation in the restructuring of that industry. In any case, such an analysis of the situation would not necessarily have spurred more militant action given the lack of institutional support for such action.

The Politics of Longwy: Conflict and Class Struggle

In contrast to the pluralistic assumptions of an underlying social consensus, the political belief system of the workers at Longwy, at least of those leading the struggle, is based on the notion that fundamental and irreconcilable conflicts of interest underlie the social order. This conception poses a society where power and resources are *cumulatively* and unequally distributed. The interests of the holders and controllers of capital dominate the political as well as the economic order which are, in fact, structurally linked in order to preserve this domination. Many Longwy workers agreed with the Usinor machinist: "You know that when one says to you here 'the bosses' that is the same thing as 'the government': That's high finance," or "[t]hose responsible are at the highest level: the government and the capitalists."[41] Those who do not possess capital are left to protect their interests by confronting the united power of capital with their numbers, their political organization, and their willingness to struggle.

For the workers at Longwy, these beliefs were confirmed by the arrival of the national riot police to protect the steel companies' property and the television relay station (which had been used to jam the broadcasts of Lorraine Cour d'Acier). The retaliatory attack on the police station where the riot police were stationed and the sacking of the Employers' Association chambers that followed were explained clearly by many workers in terms of the conflictual model:[42]

> *The CRS [riot police], they represent those in power. I was at the Employers' Association at the time of the sacking. We refused, at the CFDT, to condemn that. That symbolized the power of the bosses.*

Domination implies not only the intended consequences of the exercise of power (i.e., the intentional furthering of elite interests), but also the ability of dominant groups to withstand and externalize pressures on the society, from within or without, by passing burdens down the social hierarchy to groups with less power to avoid them. This is especially relevant to considerations of the effect of economic crisis on workers. Whatever an employer might intend, and whatever the consequences might be, the major burdens of the economic crisis will be shifted to the workers to the extent that they do not have the power to resist them.[43]

This conflictual model of politics, like the pluralist model, concerns groups. These groups, however, are stable and determined by their position in the process of production. At any given moment, an individual can only belong to one of these groups and the group to which he or she belongs greatly influences her or his interests and life chances. A Usinor welder put it more concretely: "It's the boss who holds all the power, who decides our fate. We are his slaves: we work and, in exchange, he pays us."

The relationship between these groups, called "social classes," is one of either overt or hidden conflict. The degree to which the conflict is hidden depends on the use of coercion, the threat of coercion and manipulation (i.e., on the exercise of the three faces of power) by the dominant class, and the extent to which this exercise of power is consciously confronted by politically organized and militant workers.

The workers at Longwy respond to the criticism of their illegal and often violent "strike force" tactics by pointing to the hidden violence of domination. It is the government and the bosses who have done the worst violence. As three workers put it:[44]

> *[The worker] suffers that violence in [his] whole being...[t]o be thrown into the street, to have [his] work taken away.*

> *We were born here, we have worked here and then we raised France up again after the War and suddenly, they throw everything over, the factories, billions [of francs]. And today we are called violent because we have broken two or three windows. We should be gentle? Who is violent? Is it us or them? That's what I would like to know.*

> *[t]he true violence is the closed factories, not the sacked offices.*

The interests of these groups are seen as fundamentally opposed in that they are struggling for control of the production process and of the division of labor and to realize incompatible goals for the society founded on these structures. The political consequences of this analysis seemed obvious to the Longwy workers. As the following quotes illustrate, they saw the plant closings, in part, as an effort to crush a bastion of worker militancy and left-wing politics:[45]

> *They [the capitalists] were very afraid that the working class would take power in 1978. They said to themselves: "We'll crush that." That's the reason for the Davignon Plan. You mustn't forget that in 1978, we in France were two inches away from creating a new socialist regime.*

> *Longwy is Communist. The bosses are scared stiff. They're running away.*

> *Each time a Communist mayor is elected, they tighten the screws a little more. For example, at Villerupt, Saulnes, Mont–Saint–Martin, they have all closed.*

> *To pay a workforce that has a political conscience gets too expensive for the bosses.*

The "rules of the game" exist only provisionally. They are contingent upon the relation of forces that determines whose rules obtain and to what extent they must reflect concessions to the other contending classes. The rules of the game are themselves stakes in the conflict between the classes rather than fixed and neutral standards for fair competition. In his analysis of the record of militancy at Longwy, Claude Durand concludes:[46]

> *From the time of its birth, the labor movement has affirmed itself in the illegality of the strike and the creation of unsanctioned organizations. It is by the violence of the struggles, and often through their bloody repression, that [the movement] has conquered its legitimacy.*
>
> *Once again in an order which seeks to coopt it, the labor movement appears to be able to create new social relations only through rebellion . . .*

For many Longwy workers, the struggle to preserve steel jobs in the Lorraine was only part of the larger class struggle. Even in the face of likely defeat in Longwy, the imperatives of the larger struggle were such that "[o]ur only means is to persevere, without knowing if we will win."[47]

Longwy represented a strategic turning point for the trade unions. Up until then (and particularly until 1968), despite militant rhetoric, the CGT and the CFDT left industrial policy in the hands of the political parties, the government, and the industrialists. Their concern was to reap the benefits of postwar industrial expansion and prosperity. Worker rebellions, such as in May–June 1968 and the 1974 LIP strike and occupation and its progeny, did strengthen enterprise-level movements for worker participation but were not used as levers for trade union federation involvement in national economic planning.

The economic crisis and renewed worker militancy in the face of industrial restructuring began to be seen as an opportunity for the trade unions to gain direct access to industrial decision making. Since the failure of the capitalists and their government was obvious as a result of the economic crisis and since the left-wing parties could not mount a unified challenge, the unions had to propose new policies for the production process designed to realize new societal goals.[48]

In presenting their alternative plans for the restructuring of the steel industry, the CFDT and the CGT argued for the substitution of goals related to employment, worker participation, working conditions, and social needs as the primary considerations around which industrial policies were to be built rather than around the financial exigencies of capitalists. Linking sound economic analysis to these goals won them added credibility with workers as well as the public.[49] This was a direct attack on the myth of the business climate that masked efforts to increase profitability and control of the workforce behind claims that the economic crisis dictated the industrial restructuring and the transfer of wealth and income to business and the upper class.

What the conflictual political analysis gave to the workers of Longwy and to the trade unions were strategies for identifying and piercing the mythic veil hiding the responsible authorities, detracting from worker solidarity, and shrouding alternative solutions to steel industry restructuring. It also allowed the Longwy workers' efforts to pass beyond the local level and beyond the restrictions that an unquestioned adherence to legality would necessarily have put on the movement's political impact. Most importantly, however, the conflictual analysis put the workers themselves at the center of the struggle, counting as allies only those who endorsed and followed the workers' lead. In Youngstown the struggle could and did go beyond the local level only to the extent that the efforts were not led by the workers themselves but by those who could depend on ties to powerful national organizations whose major interests did not necessarily coincide with those of workers.

The Youngstown workers' apparent quiescence stemmed in part from a pluralist politics that encouraged them to await the action of legitimate and well-connected groups such as the USWA or the churches. USWA District Director Leseganich identified this reaction without, however, noting that its cause might lie in the power continually exercised over the workers by their bosses and their union. He stated, "our people have become so lax and dependent on somebody else to do it for them, when something doesn't work, they blame somebody else."[50]

Workers themselves deplored their inaction in the face of their hopes for the success of the coalition's efforts. "[T]he clergy are all we've got," declared members of a group of older laid-off workers. "Our best bet is if they reopen the Campbell Works. We're not the only ones in the Valley. There's a lot that just sit back and don't say nothing."[51]

Conclusion: Militancy and Myth

As in the previous chapter, the conclusion of this chapter is that the recommendations of Chapter 2 are affirmed with reservations. It is clear that the French steel workers at Longwy were considerably more militant than the Youngstown workers in opposing the restructuring plans of the steel industry and the government. They had strong community support and also the unified support of the major national union confederations. They generally rejected the myths of big labor, the business climate, and legality. Their awareness and rejection of these myths allowed them to put forward and mobilize around alternative proposals for the steel industry that would preserve employment in the region. The workers themselves organized and led the struggle.

The French workers also had the support of a left-wing political alliance that had a good chance to, and in fact did, win the upcoming elections in which steel industry policy was an important issue. Both because of their ties to major political parties and because French unionism has a broad vision of its role in French life, the labor unions were able to make their message, at least with regard to job preservation, credible to a large public. In sum, the French steel workers and their unions to a large extent acted on the recommendations of Chapter 2.

In contrast, at Youngstown worker militancy was late to develop and minimal in scope, consisting of only two brief occupations of U.S. Steel offices. The workers were not in charge of the efforts to prevent the layoffs and to reopen the closed mills. Only the most militant local unions belatedly began to perform a wider role in the community—organizing the unemployed and providing relief to the unemployed, poor, and homeless. There was no unified labor support for the steel workers. Youngstown unions in other industries did not join forces to fight the steel closings. The national union leadership tended to accept the myths of big labor, the business climate, and legality. It offered no plan of its own for restructuring the steel industry. It first opposed and then gave lukewarm support to the Ecumenical Coalition's efforts and it was continually at odds with militant local unionists. This substantially weakened the efforts to oppose the closings and achieve a worker/community buyout.

Community support was fragmented. While many politicians deplored the closings and the plight of the laid-off workers, few gave strong support to the buyout plan. No political party expressly opposed or presented an alternative to the steel companies' views of industrial policy. While the Ecumenical Coalition had national contacts and conducted a national campaign, the plight of Youngstown's workers never really became a national issue. In sum, the recommendations of Chapter 2 were not followed in Youngstown.

Despite these important differences in the struggles, it cannot be said that the recommendations were conclusively borne out. It does seem clear that the greater militancy and support of the Longwy steel workers reaped certain advantages. They were able to prevent one plant closing, delay others, and avoid layoffs in most cases. Their militancy also led to the election of a left-wing government that has minimally furthered workers' rights. The failure of that government to do more for workers can in part be attributed to a decline of militancy after the election of May 1981.

The 1984 announcement of a new round of closings and job reduction in the Lorraine steel industry further clouds the evidence on the effects of the steel workers' struggle. Longwy again erupted with militancy. The militancy achieved delays and a pledge that there would be no layoffs, but again the unions were excluded from any discussion on the restructuring and financing of the steel industry. Although the socialist government has lost its credibility, workers have not fully shaken themselves out of the inaction that first the euphoria and later the disillusionment has caused. Between 1981 and 1984, French workers, despite growing unemployment and a continuing policy of austerity, were remarkably quiescent. The number of days lost to work stoppages was the lowest since World War II.[52]

Evidence for the effectiveness of militancy can also be found in Youngstown. U.S. Steel officials acknowledged that the fear of worker militancy caused them to postpone the closing of their Youngstown Works for almost two years. Newly awakened worker militancy in nearby steel communities, such as Homestead, has given rise to a serious effort to create a local steel authority and use the power of eminent domain to buy and reopen closed plants.[53]

Both the struggles at Youngstown and at Longwy resulted in the failure to prevent closings and massive job reductions. In addition, workers and their interests were excluded in the restructuring of the steel industry. The general public and governmental officials were never disabused of the myths of big labor or the business climate. Despite this, the greater militancy and support of the Longwy steel workers, based in part on their rejection of the myths, resulted in major concessions with regard to the methods of job reduction and the benefits for those affected.

Finally, while both French and American labor unions are declining in membership due to the loss of industrial jobs, this decline is neither so great nor so disastrous for the French because the unions still retain the support of a large majority of French workers when they take action. The Youngstown workers and their union suffered from their lack of militancy and community support.

Endnotes

1. James M. Perry, "Down and Out: Idle Mills, a Dearth of Hope Are Features of Ohio's Steel Towns," *Wall Street Journal*, Jan. 20, 1983, pp. 1, 14; Staughton Lynd, *The Fight Against Shutdowns: Youngstown's Steel Mill Closings* (San Pedro, Calif.: Singlejack Books, 1982), pp. 3–9; Thomas G. Fuechtmann, "Steeples and Stacks: A Case Study of the Youngstown Ecumenical Coalition" (Ph.D. diss., Univ. of Chicago, 1981), pp. 29–31; Gérard Noiriel, "Défendre l'usine secrète," *Travail* no. 4, (Apr. 1984), pp. 18–24; "Une crise structurelle aggravée par vingt ans d'errements politiques," *Le Monde*, sélection hebdomadaire, Apr. 12–18, 1984, p. 6; "Après les décisions du gouvernement sur la sidérurgie," *Le Monde*, sélection hebdomadaire, Mar. 29–Apr. 4, 1984, p. 6; For the labor history of Longwy, see generally, Gérard Noiriel, *Une autre France, Immigrés et Prolétaires à Longwy* (Paris: PUF, 1985).
2. Yves Agnes, "Le Mythe de l'acier," *Le Monde*, Oct. 12, 1980, pp. 1, 2. This and all other translations from the French are my own.
3. B. Stora, *Sidérurgie Mondiale* (Paris: Editions Economica, 1979), pp. 9, 11.
4. Youngstown workers quoted in Lynd, note 1, p. 21; Longwy steel worker quoted in Claude Durand, *Chômage et Violence* (Paris: Editions Galilée, 1981), p. 286. There is, however, a difference of tone in the reactions. The last sentence of the quoted French steel worker already sounds a note of challenge. All unnoted quotes from French workers are from this source. The translations are mine.
5. Bureau of Labor Statistics, *Major Collective Bargaining Agreements: Plant Movement, Interplant Transfer, and Relocation Allowances* (Washington, D.C.: U.S. Dept. of Labor, 1981); Fuechtman, note 1, pp. 117, 247–53; Lynd, note 1, p. 152; "Une crise structurelle," note 1; Durand, note 4, pp. 170–73.

6. Quoted in Durand, note 4, p. 70; cf. Olivier Kourchid, *Crise Économique et Modes d'Action Ouvrière* (Paris: CORDES, 1976), p. 282.

7. Paul Pakradouni, "Une nègociation peu ordinaire," *Travail*, no. 4 (Apr. 1984), pp. 12–18; Durand, note 4, pp. 161–66; Jean-Pierre Huiban, "La contraproposition industrielle comme élément de stratégie syndicale (analyse de la période 1973–80)," 2 vols. (Doctoral diss., Univ. de Paris IX, 1981), vol. 1, pp. 185–87; Terry Buss and F. S. Redburn, *Shutdown at Youngstown* (Albany: State Univ. of New York Press, 1983), p. 22; Lynd, note 1, pp. 67–74, 95–105, 170–72.

8. Olivier Kourchid, "Luttes ouvrières dans la sidérurgie en France et aux U.S.A.: Autonomie et contraintes à Longwy (Lorraine) et à Youngstown (Ohio)," paper delivered to the 10th World Sociological Congress, Mexico, Aug. 1982.

9. Lynd, note 1, pp. 49–56.

10. Pakradouni, note 7; Huiban, note 7, pp. 162–83; Gérard Noiriel, *Vivre et Lutter à Longwy* (Paris: Maspero, 1980). The two federations differed substantially on the amount of the projected increase in production as well as the effect of productivity increases on employment. The CGT projected higher production increases and maintained that these and the productivity improvements would allow for the reduction of working hours without reduction in jobs or pay. The CFDT, with a greater acceptance of the notion of market saturation, assumed that increased productivity would mean some loss of steel employment to be compensated for by early retirement and the creation of new downstream industrial jobs, linked to improved steel production, in branches such as construction, automobiles, and machine tools.

11. Durand, note 4, p. 132.

12. Statement of Lloyd McBride to the House Ways and Means Committee, Subcommittee on Trade, Sept. 20, 1977.

13. This chronology and the following descriptions of events at Longwy come from Durand (note 4), Noiriel *Travail* (note 1), and Huiban (note 7) and interviews with Longwy steel workers. General information about the French steel industry comes form Stora, note 3, and Michel Freyssenet, *La Sidérurgie Française* (Paris: Editions Savelli, 1979).

14. Fuechtman, note 1, pp. 119–24.

15. The description of events at Youngstown come primarily from Fuechtman (note 1), Buss and Redburn (note 7), and Lynd, (note 1). The possibility of an alternative, privately owned use of the Campbell Works, was eliminated when a local Youngstown, Sheet & Tube executive acknowledged that the Lykes Corporation had been trying unsuccessfully to find a buyer for some time. Fuechtman, pp. 149–50. Unnoted quotes are from Lynd, note 1.

16. Kourchid, "Luttes ouvrieres," note 8, p. 13.

17. A phasing plan, not unlike Sullivan's, later became a part of the revised UDAG and EDA fund applications prepared by NCEA, Gar Alperovitz and Jeff Faux, "The Youngstown Project," in Frank Lindenfeld and Joyce Rothschild–Whitt (eds.), *Workplace Democracy and Social Change* (Boston: Porter Sargent, 1982), pp. 353–69.

18. The comment of a worker in the laminating mill is quoted in Durand, note 4, p. 135.

19. The organizations joining the struggle on behalf of the workers included the Women's Action Committee (which remained active on women's issues and became the Committee on Contraception, Abortion, and Sexuality), the Committee of the Flames of Hope (organized by primary and secondary school teachers), the Intercantonal Business Action Committee (made up of artisans and merchants of the region), and a Youth Action Committee.

20. See generally Richard Sennett and Jonathan Cobb, *The Hidden Injuries of Class* (New York: Vintage, 1973), which investigates the many forms and sources of American working-class feelings of incompetence and lack of worth when faced with an educated elite and problems of an intellectual nature.

21. Olivier Kourchid, *Les Ouvriers entre la Crise et l'Entreprise* (Paris: Groupe de Sociologie du Travail, 1984), pp. 319–66. The quote and supporting tables are found on pp. 258–60. These surveys were not done in Youngstown and Longwy. The comparison was between workers in and around Los Angeles with workers in and around Paris.

22. Gerald Dickey quoted in Lynd, note 1, pp. 27–28.

23. Kourchid, "Luttes ouvrières," note 8, p. 2.

24. For a more elaborate comparison and contrast of these differing conceptions and their consequences, see William Connolly, "Theoretical Self-Consciousness," in W. Connolly and G. Gordon, *Social Structure and Political Theory* (Lexington, Mass.: D.C. Heath, 1974), pp. 40–68 and Fred Dallmayr, "Empirical Political Theory and the Image of Man," *Polity*, 2 (1970), pp. 443–65.

25. Quoted in Fuechtman, supra, pp. 226–7; cf. Buss and Redburn, p. 26.

26. The editorial opinion of the *Youngstown Vindicator*, Feb. 19, 1977, quoted in Fuechtman, note 1, p. 225.

27. John Greenman quoted in Fuechtman, note 1, p. 260.

28. Interview with James Smith, January 1980, quoted in Fuechtman, note 1, p. 245.

29. Letter of Lloyd McBride to President Carter, May 16, 1979, quoted in Fuechtman, note 1, p. 246.

30. Lynd, note 1, p. 187.

31. *Local 1330 et al.* v. *U.S. Steel, Proceedings Had Before the Honorable Thomas D. Lambros*, Feb. 28, 1980, pp. 9–12, quoted in Lynd, note 1, pp. 164–66 and *Local 1330, USWA* v. *U.S. Steel*, 492 F.Supp 1, 10 (N.D. Ohio 1980).

32. Kay Schlozman and Sidney Verba, *Injury to Insult: Unemployment, Class, and Political Response* (Cambridge, Mass.: Harvard Univ. Press, 1979), p. 265. This, of course, is a substantial challenge to pluralist theory unless one assumes that the unemployed are on some basis justifiably excluded from political decision making (i.e. they are not a "legitimate" group).

33. Quoted in Lynd, note 1, p. 79.

34. Quoted in Lynd, note 1, p. 68.

35. Buss and Redburn, note 7, p. 188.

36. Quoted in Fuechtman, note 1, p. 346.

37. Letters to the Editor, *Brier Hill Unionist*, March–April 1979, quoted in Lynd, note 1, pp. 125–26; cf. Stanley Aronowitz, *False Promises* (New York: McGraw–Hill, 1973), pp. 214–62 and Sumner Rosen, "The U.S.: A Time for Reassessment," in Solomon Barkin (ed.), *Worker Militancy and Its Conse-*

quences (New York: Praeger, 1975). For an analysis of the failures of the pluralist conception of collective bargaining, see Katherine Stone, "The Post-War Paradigm in American Labor Law," *Yale Law Journal*, 90 (1981), pp. 1509–52.

38. Quoted in Charles Lally, "Praise God and Pass the Federal Aid," *Akron Beacon*, May 21, 1978, p. 10 and cited in Fuechtman, note 1, p. 236.

39. See e.g. William Connolly, *The Terms of Political Discourse* (Lexington, Mass.: D.C. Heath, 1974), ch. 2 and C. B. MacPherson, "The Economic Penetration of Political Theory," *Journal of the History of Ideas* 39 (Jan.–Mar. 1978), pp. 101–18.

40. The letter is found in Fuechtman, note 1, pp. 369–76.

41. Durand, note 4, p. 114.

42. Ibid., p. 58.

43. The description of the conflictual model is adopted from Connolly, "Theoretical Self-Consciousness," note 24, pp. 47–55. The issue of whether the production of unintended consequences is a mark of power is an important one with regard to research methodology. From the standpoint of political action, the conflictual model avoids the tendency toward fatalism and inaction which the pluralist model encourages in cases where no strictly intended consequences of elite action are easily identified as the cause of a grievance. For example, the acceptance of the conflictual analysis makes irrelevant whether Ronald Reagan was really a "nice guy." Instead, the effect of the policies he supports or merely allows to operate would be the basis of the evaluation.

44. Durand, note 4, p. 49, 56.

45. Ibid., pp. 116–17.

46. Ibid., pp. 45–46.

47. Ibid., p. 150.

48. Huiban, note 7, pp. 12–33.

49. Ibid., pp. 160–78.

50. From an interview quoted in Fuechtman, note 1, p. 250.

51. From an article in the *Youngstown Vindicator*, Mar. 25, 1979, quoted in Fuechtman, note 1, p. 248; cf. Schlozman and Verba, note 32, p. 264, who conclude that the unemployed are politically unorganized and inactive because other organizations, such as unions, claim to act for them rather than with them and do not encourage the unemployed to become politically active themselves.

52. Catherine Lévy, "Crise des organisations syndicales et politiques patronales," *Travail*, no. 4 (Apr. 1984), pp. 28–32; Michel Noblecourt, "La déprime des syndicats," *Le Monde*, sélection hebdomadaire, Feb. 28–Mar. 6, 1985, p. 8; "Sollac: menace de paralysie totale," *Le Républicain Lorrain*, Nov. 21, 1984, pp. 1, B; Eric Le Boucher, "Les restructurations un an àpres," *Le Monde*, sélection hebdomadaire, Mar. 15–20, 1985, p. 11.

53. Tamar Lewin, "Factory Takeover Weighed by City," *New York Times*, June 5, 1984, p. 1; Charles Craypo, "The Deindustrialization of a Factory Town," in Donald Kennedy (ed.), *Labor and Reindustrialization* (University Park: Pennsylvania State Univ., Dept. of Labor Studies, 1984), pp. 63–64; Lynd, note 1, p. 212. Conversations with Ron Weisen, president of USWA Local #1397, Homestead, Penn.

Chapter 5

CONCLUSION: POWER, POLITICS, AND PLANT CLOSINGS

In Chapter 1, we raised several questions that would be explored, if not answered, through the evidence brought forward in this book. These questions, which concern the American response to plant closings, were: Why has the drastic assault on their economic well-being that plant closings and economic layoffs represent not spurred workers to greater political and trade union militancy? Why have workers, their unions, and communities not been more active in pressing politically for plant closing and layoff regulation? When undertaken, why have such efforts been so half-hearted? Why have such efforts not captured the imagination and support of most U.S. trade unionists? Why are the reactions of workers, their unions, and communities so different in the United States from those of other Western industrialized countries?

Our search for the answers to these questions has focused on the exercise of power by business interests. The evidence suggests that workers and unions simply do not have the political clout to challenge business in an area where it is directly interested. The law, the economic power, and the votes are on the side of business when it comes to the question of how and where business should invest its resources. The lack of worker militancy on this issue is simply a recognition of the impossibility of countering the power of business. The recent history of labor's political agenda has borne out the conclusion that political successes

167

have been achieved rarely and then only with the help of other groups or the acquiescence of business interests.

On the other hand, the comparison with France (or other European countries where plant closing and layoff regulations exist) indicates that workers can extract gains on these issues from strong business interests. This poses anew the questions asked earlier. One clear point that arises from the foregoing analysis is that the American labor movement (and some have questioned whether there still is a movement) has not been as politically militant in pursuing its goals as the French labor movement. For that matter, although they have made gains in periods of militancy, French workers have also been hurt when that militancy subsides.

We have attributed the loss of militancy largely to the hidden faces of power. One of these hidden faces is the power to set the public political agenda and to suppress or impede the full public exposure of certain issues and grievances. (This is what we have called the second face of power—the first face, the public face, is not hidden.) Maneuvering, deception, and outright repression kept secret the facts and decisions leading up to the plant closings at Youngstown and Longwy. These decisions were not scrutinized or debated by the public or the workers directly affected. The decisions with regard to investments and operations often created the conditions that later served as the arguments put forward for the closings. Even after the closings were announced, the companies and the governments were successful in restricting the debate and clouding the responsibilities. This was often achieved by the use of myths; that is, self-serving justifications of the plans of the steel industry having emotional appeal, but little supporting evidence. Without knowledge of important decisions being made, without the requisite corporate information, and without someone to confront, militancy is difficult to generate.

The lack of militancy of American workers can also be attributed to the third face of power: the adoption and internalization by workers and the public of the myths put forward to serve the interests of business. The belief in these myths by American workers or their leaders deprived them of alternative economic and political explanations for the catastrophic events affecting them. Without such an explanation, they could not mobilize a solid and militant opposition. Public belief in these myths deprived workers of the support of their communities and of public officials for a militant opposition to plant closings and the power of business interests. Even for the French workers who rejected the myths and had alternative proposals, the acceptance of the myths by the public made their task more difficult and greatly added to the power of business and government to reject the workers' demands.

The Myth of Big Labor

The myth of big labor discredits the efforts of workers to improve their condition by collective action, and, at the same time, lulls workers into complacency about the extent of their power and the extent to which business and government take their interests into account. The myth declares that organized labor has excessive political and economic power and that such power is unnecessary for the protection of workers' interests and detrimental to the interests of unorganized workers and the public. The power of trade unions is portrayed as an unnecessary burden on business activities which hampers the ability of affected businesses to compete with foreign and nonunion enterprises. Furthermore, union leadership is viewed as economically irresponsible, corrupt, and authoritarian.

Employers used this myth extensively in their efforts to squelch plant closing legislation in the United States. Through constant repetition and wide-spread media coverage, this myth has become fixed in the consciousness of the public, including trade unionists themselves. Many in Youngstown regarded the steel closings as a mixed blessing because they broke the power of the USWA in the region. In recent years, the myth has gained credence among French young people. This has had the effect of boosting the membership of the less militant confederations at the expense of the more militant CGT and CFDT. The complacency that the myth can generate may account for the drop in militancy among French workers since the election of 1981 which brought the "workers' government" into power.

The acceptance of this myth has had a two-fold effect on unions. First, it has restricted them to making only negotiable demands. These are demands that can, and generally will, be compromised and also demands that do not challenge the legitimate existence of the other side; that is, capital. Yet, the myth itself challenges the legitimate existence of unions and collective action. Thus, at Youngstown the USWA did not support and often tried to suppress the militant trade unionists who were working for the Community Steel buyout plan. At Longwy, the FO, other conservative unions, and ultimately the CFDT agreed to bargain on the methods of job reduction despite the desires of local members to continue the struggle for an alternative restructuring plan.

The second effect of the unions' acceptance of the myth of big labor is that they enter into cooperation with business to force workers to honor the agreements even when they may not be in the workers' interest. The complicity of the UAW leadership and General Motors (GM) management in imposing discipline on wildcat strikers in the early seventies is well known. Much of the friction between the USWA leadership and militant steel workers in Youngstown and Pittsburgh stems originally from the "no strike" provisions and cooperative efforts instituted in the Experimental Negotiating Agreement of 1973. In France, the CFDT has dissolved a local union at Usinor Dunkerque because of its refusal to accept a nationally negotiated agreement on the effects of job reductions in the steel industry. The negative effect of such actions on worker militancy is evident.

The Myth of the Business Climate

The myth of the business climate declares that any action by government, popular movements, or workers to regulate or restrict business activities is an illegitimate burden on the right of property and the profitability of business. Such a burden is held to reduce the attractiveness of investment in the jurisdiction (city, state, region, country) in which the action is taken. It is not difficult to see how the acceptance of this myth discourages plant closing legislation, worker participation in establishing steel industry policy, and worker militancy.

The term "business climate" signifies a range of political factors affecting the control businesses have over their workforce and their environment. Under this rubric, businesses solicit bids for political submissiveness from states and cities. Bluestone and Harrison recount the story of Goodyear's move from Akron, Ohio, to Lawton, Oklahoma, before which Goodyear had solicited bids from six communities stating bluntly that it would accept the best bid. Lawton not only made tax concessions but had school district lines redrawn, an interstate highway moved, and access roads built. While many jurisdictions are offering tax breaks and cleared land to attract businesses, New York is the only state to have thoroughly studied its economic incentive program—and has repealed it. Not only was it found that the economic incentives were not really determinative for business location, but businesses that had accepted public funds, such as Otis Elevator in Yonkers, had not necessarily remained in the state.[1]

The business climate myth masks more than raids on the public treasury for private gain. It masks efforts to transfer wealth from the poor and the working class to corporate treasuries. States have been driven to reduce their welfare, workers' compensation, and unemployment benefit programs in order to lessen business tax burdens and reduce the "social wage," seen by business as keeping up wages and heightening workers' resistance to the demands of business. In addition, a good business climate signifies little or no efforts to protect the rights of workers to organize, the environment, workers' health and safety, and the rights of women and minorities. The political nature of business climate decisions has been revealed in recent lawsuits where evidence has come to light of the use of racial composition and the extent of trade union activity as criteria in corporate location decisions.[2]

Michael Storper and Richard Walker suggest the interplay of the political and economic aspects of a business location decision. Different industrial processes raise different political considerations. In the mechanized processing of industries such as cotton textiles, specific but easily learned skills are required to set up, run, and feed large machines. The work is hard, rapidly paced, and repetitive. Competitive pressures on the industry are great and profits are low. Given the prospects of low pay, job insecurity, and extremely gruelling work, turnover will be high unless a highly dependent workforce can be found or created. These industries, often situated in rural North and South Carolina, draw workers from captive rural and small town labor markets where geographic mobility is low and political activism and labor militancy are not part of the traditional rural values. Management tends to work with existing local elites to maintain the political quiescence of the populace. Internally, management relies on segmenting the labor force through piecework standards, often utilizing racial and sexual divisions as well.[3]

The political meaning of a favorable business climate is best brought home when considering the global mobility of capital. Those Third World countries hailed as the great economic successes of recent years (e.g., Singapore, Taiwan, and South Korea) are characterized by an impoverished working class that earns an average of less than $1.00 per hour with little or no fringe benefits. Job security is low, and the employer is generally unrestricted in dealing with the workforce. Labor–management relations, where anything of the sort can be said to exist, are heavily weighted in favor of management by the repressive power of the state. Political rights are restricted for the entire population, but most especially for the working class. Despite the growing absenteeism in many industrial operations, the political docility of the Singapore worker is evident in this comment on the upcoming parliamentary elections: "If we need an opposition, the Government will give us one."[4]

These are considered the successes in that economic growth has been rapid and some of that growth has trickled down to the worker. The failures are too numerous to list. The failure of capital investment to greatly benefit workers is not a concern for businesses seeking a favorable business climate. If an adequate, cheap labor force exists and the government can assure, by whatever political means, the security of the investment, then capital will move toward that country.

The appeal of sources of cheap labor is an important aspect of the threat of foreign competition from low-wage countries. In the United States, this foreign competition is not really foreign at all—30% of it comes from subsidiaries of American multinationals, and at least another 20% comes from American investment in majority foreign-owned companies. France and the United States are two of the eight countries that control 95% of the foreign investments in the world. Foreign investment enhances control of the workforce in two ways. It allows firms to play off one set of workers against another in transferring production to the lowest paid and most docile workforce, and it creates the "foreign competition" that allows business to suppress and channel the political demands of the home country workers. The business climate myth protects the mobility of capital. Workers are outflanked by the movement of capital whose control and origin is hidden from the public.[5]

In the cases we studied, the linked notions of a favorable business climate and the danger of foreign competition served to isolate workers and their demands from the wider public support they needed. Public officials accepted these notions and worked to forestall state and federal plant closing legislation in the United States. In France, the right linked these notions to the balance of payments deficits that the country suffered after 1974. This clearly heightened business and government opposition to extending the rights workers had gained in the 1969 accord on economic layoffs and the 1974 renewal of that accord. In particular, the Law of January 3, 1975 did nothing to limit the destabilizing of employment by subcontracting, fixed period contracts, and manpower service workers.

The socialist government elected in 1981 also succumbed to these notions and the capital flight that they hide. Despite election promises to curb the destabilization of employment, to reduce the hours of work without loss of pay, to raise the social wage, and to promote worker self-management, timid initial experiments along these lines were soon canceled and a policy of austerity to reduce imports and reduce charges on business was adopted. In the name of foreign competition, the socialist government cut steel employment in the Lorraine, giving rise to a new round of violence and protests.

The steel industry, which was the focus of the struggles at Youngstown and Longwy, has used the threat of foreign competition as a major weapon to control and reduce the costs of its workforce. The workings of the business climate myth and the third face of power are particularly evident in the United States where the USWA has been a vehicle for conveying the industry's view to the rank and file and channeling worker demands into a cooperative relationship with management. In the 1950s, the USWA had rejected this same argument when the steel companies had justified their calls for wage moderation by citing the threat of foreign competition. In 1959, the year of a major steel strike, the USWA had published a pamphlet, "The Foreign Competition Hoax," in which high profits and prices were blamed for foreign penetration.[6]

The myth of the business climate links the foreign competition hoax to the notion, which when baldly stated seems contradictory, that workers must accept the sacrifice of their jobs and their

salaries to protect employment and their standard of living. Myth
portrays sacrifice in the particular as preservation in the abstract.
For example, the president of the major French employers' association *Confédération Nationale du Patronat Français* has argued
that the legal constraints on economic layoffs deprived employers
of "the means for meshing the solution to labor problems with the
economic constraints of our time . . . so that our firms, more competitive in a more coherent economy, will be able to assure their
employees true security and a real improvement in their standards of living."[7]

The Myth of Legality

The myth of legality declares that the legal system is neutral, fair,
and timely in its handling of issues that affect workers; that the
law's sense of justice reflects the same values as workers' sense of
justice; and that the law "means what it says." This book has
presented evidence that this conception is a myth and that this
myth saps worker militancy. Willingness to exceed legal limitations on labor action was an important reason for the gains that
French workers achieved legislatively and politically. The law
itself, as in the case of the French administrative layoff procedures, works on behalf of workers when they mobilize to use the
law as a political instrument.

The acceptance of the myth of legality is to accept an abstraction in place of something solid and effective. Workers' or trade
unions' rights are abstractions that mask the realities of the workplace. To have a right to organize sounds grand, but it does not
mean that one has an effective organization. To have the right to
bargain collectively does not mean that one has the power to
reach an acceptable agreement or that the agreement will be
enforced as intended.

In both France and the United States, there is a double barrier
between the abstraction and the everyday practice. The first
barrier is economic and political power. Because workers' rights
are procedural rather than substantive, they merely enable
organization, bargaining, and collective agreements. Workers can
avail themselves of these rights only if they have the power to
make them work. Where they do not have the power, as is the case

for the majority of workers in both countries, they must rely either on the goodwill of employers or on the state. There is little evidence for the unforced and nonarbitrary benevolence of employers, particularly in times of economic crisis.

To rely on the state is to confront directly the third face of power. Labor law in both France and the United States is seen as an overlay upon a much older and more firmly established system of law that secures the rights of property and establishes the relationship between masters and servants. Every point of labor law, then, is shaded by the underlying legal notions. Where labor law is silent, the earlier notions control. The earlier legal notions are seen as the foundations of modern society and branded into the national consciousness, while labor law is seen as a matter of positive adjustment to specific and contingent conditions. Workers trying for recognition of their interests in the legal system must, like the Red Queen in *Alice in Wonderland*, run as fast as they can just to stay where they are.

The second barrier is the danger that legal and administrative procedures will be taken as defining the limits of worker action for the workers themselves. It may be comforting for workers to assume that the abstract statements of their rights, being vague and subject to interpretation, contain in fact all that they hope to achieve. It is easy to move from this to the equally comforting notion that once the courts or the appropriate administrative agencies have been invoked, workers' problems are as good as solved. Even at the level of major changes in administrations and policies, it is dangerous to assume, as French workers have so recently learned, that the election of a government dependent on workers' support will realize workers' goals.

It is important that legal remedies for workers' grievances be regarded in three ways. The first is that they are political tests that measure and, if favorable, add to the relationship of political forces. The second is that the law be used as a tool to protect and extend worker militancy. The law can help to protect the organizers, organizing, and organizations of workers by creating procedures and hurdles that any attack on workers and their political activities must overcome. Given the existing relationship of forces, the law can serve in this manner only as a way to delay and impede but not to prevent or blunt efforts by the controllers of capital to control the lives of workers.

Worker Militancy Versus Capital Mobility:
Fighting for Democracy

The power of business has propelled French and American workers into a wider and deeper struggle than they had originally intended. Proposed and enacted plant closing and layoff legislation and the struggles at Longwy and Youngstown overflowed the confines of traditional labor politics. The workers opposed the mobility of capital which imposed upon them a community-destroying mobility. In its broadest sense, the mobility of the worker encompasses all of the attributes that make his or her human capacities available and submissive to the needs of a production process that others control, thus turning the worker into "human capital."[8]

While such a resistance naturally touched on worker access to corporate information and worker participation in investment and production decisions, it focused on the preservation of jobs and plants in their original communities and the maintenance and improvement of job skills and working conditions already in place. This resistance to geographic and downward skill mobility (i.e., to plant closings, layoffs, transfers, off-the-job retraining, and community destruction) points up a new stage in the struggle between capital and labor. The fact that both French and American workers were unprepared for this new level of conflict suggests some of the reasons why the workers at Youngstown and Longwy failed to achieve their ends against the power of the corporations and government.

This stage of the struggle resembles a war. Many writers and journalists have already noted that the mobilizations and dislocation caused by the mobility of capital are similar to those that occur in wartime. It is clear that a major plant closing has devastating effects on mental and physical health, on family and social relationships, and on personal and community finances. One can see the shells of deserted and vandalized buildings, abandoned houses, and the lines of people seeking food, shelter, and social services. One can see as well the exodus of economic refugees toward other less disastrously affected towns and regions.

The mobilization, regimentation, and deployment of the home and captive workforces in wartime is analogous to the business ideal of an infinitely mobile and politically docile workforce that can be treated as just another commodity or productive resource—that is, as human capital available when, where, and as needed.[9] The secrecy surrounding the decisions to close and the lack of concern for the interests of workers at Youngstown certainly resembled the treatment of a captive workforce in wartime. So too does the attempt to suppress worker demands by resorting to calls for patriotic sacrifice (by workers, not owners) in order to beat foreign countries.

It appears that in some ways the captains of industry have learned the lesson of modern warfare better than the captains of armies. That lesson concerns the primacy of mobility. Those who must defend centers of population and their social and political networks are at a disadvantage in a war of movement. The advantage goes to those who can abandon the towns and cities and who can isolate their opponents from the support of the general population. This is exactly what business is doing.

The workers of a Youngstown or a Longwy are simply outflanked as capital moves away from centers of population and, in particular, from centers of active and democratic political organization. In the end, politically organized workers are isolated from the rest of the population by the flight of capital and the use of myth. The "hearts and minds" of the population are turned against any political organization that challenges the interests of business. Unorganized workers are placed in the "fortified hamlets" of suburban, rural, and Third World industrial and office facilities.

In the United States, firms and jobs are moving to less populous areas of the country. This strategy is manifested in the flight of capital from the large cities to the suburbs and the countryside, from the regions of high population density to those less densely populated, from the Northeast to the South and West, and from the United States to the Third World. For example, between 1969 and 1978 in 36 states (of the 48 for which comparable data were available), the rate of growth of industrial employment of the largest city of the state was less than the growth in industrial employment for the entire state. In 12 states, the rate of growth for the state was positive while that of the largest city was negative. There is also a strong negative correlation between the rate of growth of industrial employment and the population density of the state.[10]

An analogous tendency exists in France. With only a few exceptions, large cities are losing industrial employment to the suburbs and to other less densely populated regions. Between 1975 and 1978, 6 of the 8 most densely populated regions in France suffered a loss of industrial jobs while 10 of the 14 regions of less than the average population density gained industrial employment. This trend has been confirmed by recent studies and by the latest French census.[11] As noted in Chapters 2 and 3, when the location of industrial jobs changes, there is also a diminution in their number, their stability, their remuneration, and the extent that they are unionized. In particular, many of the new industrial jobs are temporary or with small subcontractors.[12]

The same thing is occurring in the United States and in France, as well as in other industrialized countries. There is a flight, and threat of flight, of capital from the cities, regions, and nations where democratic and participatory political organization is strong or growing and raises demands that threaten the needs of capital. The flight is not only from the demands of workers, but also from those of environmentalists, racial and ethnic minorities, women, and the the young. Business flees the threat of a demo-cratization of the economic and financial decisions it considers its prerogatives. This is a major reason why "greenfield" develop-ment (the location of new of modernized facilities in areas with-out a significant industrial history or implantation) is preferred to "brownfield" development (the reimplantation of industrial facil-ities in older industrial areas) even where the direct economic costs of greenfield development are greater. This is also the reason why it was necessary to crush the worker and community resistance to the mobility of capital at Youngstown and Longwy. There the demands of several groups—workers, clergy, mer-chants, and public servants—began to coalesce and take political shape that implied limitations on capital.

What business faced in the sixties and the seventies, more evidently in France than in the United States, was a potential convergence of labor struggles in the workplace with other demands for citizen access to economic decision making. Manuel Castells has noted that "the politicization of urban problems" developed new modes of conflict and new contradictions at the interior of the bourgeoisie in the form of the humanist and refor-mist opposition to the immediate demands of business. It has already been shown that the struggle at Youngstown took up these modes of conflict. In Longwy, the movement of the struggle from the plants to the streets of Paris and the Lorraine with a great deal of community support represented the threat of a popular countermobilization resisting the mobility of capital. In both cases, the state ultimately showed its links with capital by aiding in suppression of these movements.[13]

The multinationalization of production, the closings and transfers of operations, and the creation of parallel production units in expectation of a transfer, figure significantly in the strategy of business for escaping democratic countermobilization. If a firm is able to move to areas of a country where that countermobilization has not developed because strong, participatory political organizations do not exist, that firm may be able to structure the social and economic space according to its needs. One French analyst has aptly described this phenomenon with regard to the Touraine region:[14]

> *Employment only comes to Tours following an industrial and financial logic which local leaders have not grasped. . . . [Businesses] come to the Touraine not to develop, but to appropriate to themselves just those characteristics of a previously under-industrialized region.*

The U.S. automobile industry looks to rural Tennessee and Ohio. The French steel industry looks to Fos and Neuves–Maisons. At the same time, the threat of such moves serves to disorganize existing industrial communities. Kellogg Co. imposes governmental consolidation on Battle Creek by threatening to move its operations if the required referendum is not proposed and passed. Detroit destroys Poletown for GM's new Cadillac plant using special "quick take" eminent domain procedures. Longwy workers view the Lorraine plant closings as the response of capital to their electoral support of the left.

Similarly, investment and relocation in other countries where the government has hindered, often by repressive measures, the development of strong, participatory political organizations and active labor movements is another aspect of the use of the mobility of capital to externalize and ignore all needs other than its own. Investment in Taiwan, Mexico, Korea, Singapore, Brazil, and South Africa is thus doubly effective in securing capital from political challenge. In those countries, the labor force and political organizations are tightly controlled in the interests of capital. The resulting lower cost production (i.e., of the costs internalized by the firm) and international trade advantage provide a powerful threat for confronting the political challenges of organized groups in the home countries.

Militancy and Democracy: Dangers and Hopes

In the early seventies, groups of French and American workers directly confronted the third face of power. These confrontations were fueled by militant actions at Lordstown, LIP, and Rateau that, in turn, helped motivate future militancy. At the Lordstown, Ohio, GM plant in 1972, young workers resisted management speed-up and threatened layoffs by slowdowns, sabotage, and working to rule. They were at the same time asserting a system of informal self-control of the production process. Although union officials and many older workers disapproved of these militant actions, the success in forcing management to retreat and the widespread publicity given these actions raised the hopes of a new militancy among workers. The new militancy would be based in part on the modes of action found in the antiwar and civil rights movements.

At the LIP Watch Company, threatened layoffs and reductions in operations moved the workers to occupy their plant in order "to safeguard the tools of production" and to continue operations under their own control. This early occupation spawned a wave of similar militant actions. The initial public support for these actions gave a boost to the parties of the left and even forced changes in labor law.

Workers had rejected the prevailing productivist economic ideology and the myths of big labor, the business climate, and legality. They maintained that workers were not merely factors of production but that production was meaningless unless it created a worklife providing psychological, social, and economic fulfillment. The initial successes encouraged the belief that a radical transformation of work was possible and that this transformation would give workers more control over the process and end results of production. Furthermore, it encouraged the belief that public consciousness could be changed to accept what were essentially new notions of democracy and property. This was a utopian moment.

What French and American workers have since discovered is that a change in consciousness cannot last without continued militant struggle and institutional supports for that struggle. The third face of power and its myths both support and are supported by power in its other, more concrete forms. Prevailing institutions and ideologies have deep resources, including the use of police and military force, to maintain their domination. This realization can be profoundly disillusioning to those who have experienced the utopian moment.

In particular, capital's power to segment and divide the workforce has increased by playing off one group of workers against another—unionized vs. nonunionized, domestic vs. foreign, intellectual vs. manual, skilled vs. unskilled, men vs. women, employed vs. unemployed, young vs. old, white vs. black, industrial vs. nonindustrial, Northeastern vs. Southwestern.[15] Unions have not yet been able to come to grips with these divisions. Neither have other, even socialist, political movements successfully challenged them. A new labor militancy is necessary—one that reaches out to other groups and that sees the links between the workplace and the community, and between capital and government policy, both foreign and domestic. A new democratic politics must be forged that can overcome both these divisions and the attack on democracy that business is masking with its myths.

A Final Look at the Recommendations

The recommendations originally made in Chapter 2 called for increased worker militancy, increased unionization and solidarity, and the development of political unions. Together these efforts would help establish the institutional supports for a new democratic labor militancy. The details of the recommendations were:

Worker Militancy

1. Development of new and more militant tactics for waging labor struggles; for example, occupations, boycotts, demonstrations, partial and temporary work stoppages, negative advertising, and embarrassing executives and investors.
2. Greater encouragement and aid from union headquarters to local militants.
3. Worker support for nonunion militant action for restrictions on the prerogatives of capital; for example, with regard to environmental protection, racism, sexism, bribery of foreign officials, and divestiture from oppressive countries.
4. Major union campaigns for access to corporate information, and worker participation in management and against "no-strike" agreements and management prerogatives.

5. Wage or staffing concessions for businesses in real difficulty only where there has been a full disclosure of corporate information and significant concessions on management prerogatives.

Unionization and Solidarity

6. Labor unionism and solidarity as a lifetime commitment to bettering lives of past, present, and future workers.
7. No tiered compensation or pension agreements.
8. More union services to members and *nonmembers;* a move toward cultural unionism.
9. Retention of retired and unemployed members in the union.
10. New forms of union-linked associations designed to assist nonmembers and prospective members among the unemployed, the retired, women, minorities, families of union members; more attention to the needs of and special associations for clerical, office, sales, and service workers.
11. Revival of and greater role for coworker selected stewards at the shop, office, and workplace; personal attention to the problems of individual workers.
12. An end to high salaries, large offices, and executive-style "perks" for union officials that identify them more with management than with the rank and file; worker's wages plus expenses for union work.
13. Greater reliance on volunteers to do important union work; payment of lost wages and expenses only.

Political Unionism

14. Direct attack on the myths of big labor, the business climate, and legality; portrayal of unions as progressive workers' organizations for improving life with a special concern for those who are powerless as individuals.
15. More community outreach and opening up of internal processes to members of the local community.
16. Union adoption of a massive "What are bosses for?" campaign in the media and in schools to counteract business mythology; public awareness that workers are fully capable of organizing their own productive activities.
17. A national daily newspaper and regular national exposure on TV and radio in documentaries, news, and drama to

show the realities and the worth of workers' lives, their work, and their organizations.

18. Institution of labor history, taught from labor's viewpoint, as a required part of the curriculum in elementary and secondary schools.
19. Creation of strong ties with all progressive movements that challenge the power of capital over the lives of human beings; that is, with groups opposing racism, sexism, and U.S. foreign and military policy (interventionism and support of repressive governments) and with groups fighting for environmental protection, consumer protection, aid to the poor, comparable worth, economic democracy, and civil rights.
20. Use of pension funds for politically conscious investments.
21. Promotion of stronger ties with foreign workers and their unions, not to further U.S. foreign policy, but to further workers' interests internationally.
22. Creation of a left-wing political party as a forum to challenge the conventional political and economic wisdom of the Democrats and the Republicans, to bring workers' interests forward, and to support more militant labor politics.

The evidence presented in this book clearly supports these recommendations. While it is a controversial and idealistic program for change in labor politics, the recommendations are based on the need for greater militancy, greater solidarity, and greater political consciousness. Without a strong workers' movement, allied with other progressive movements that confront the interests of capital, more than jobs, unions, and wages are in jeopardy. Democracy and human lives hang in the balance.

Endnotes

1. Barry Bluestone and Bennett Harrison, *The Deindustrialization of America* (New York: Basic Books, 1982), pp. 183–84; Lawrence J. Tell, "Plant Shutdowns: The Cities Fight," *New York Times*, May 15, 1983, pp. F8–9.
2. Reginald Stuart, "Businesses Said To Have Barred New Plants in Largely Black Communities," *New York Times*, Feb. 15, 1983, p. A14.
3. Michael Storper and Richard Walker, "The Spatial Division of Labor: Labor and the Location of Industries," in L. Sawers and W. Tabb, *Sunbelt/Snowbelt* (New York: Oxford Univ. Press, 1984), pp. 36–37.
4. Barbara Crossette, "Leader's Foes Gird for Fight in Singapore," *New York Times*, Oct. 14, 1984, p. 19.

5. William Goldsmith, "Bringing the Third World Home: Enterprise Zones for America?" in Sawers and Tabb, note 2, pp. 344–48; Julien Savary, *Les Multinationales Francaises* (Paris: Presses Univesitaires de France, 1981), pp. 163–66; Jacqueline Grapin, "Les stratégies des firmes multinationales," *Le Monde Dimanche*, Feb. 2, 1982, p.XI; cf. Bluestone and Harrison, note 1, pp. 42–64, 170–78; see generally, Richard Barnet and Ronald Müller, *Global Reach* (New York: Simon & Schuster, 1973).

6. Staughton Lynd, *The Flight Against Shutdowns: Youngstown's Steel Mill Closings* (San Pedro, Calif.: Singlejack Book, 1982), p. 50.

7. *Le Monde*, Jan. 17, 1979, p. 34.

8. Jean-Paul De Gaudemar, *Mobilité du Travail et Accumlation du Capital* (Paris: Maspero, 1976), pp. 257–58.

9. This general idea was suggested to me by Jean-Paul De Gaudemar, *La Mobilisation Générale* (Paris: Editions du Champs Urbain, 1979). See e.g., Bluestone and Harrison, note, 1, Ch. 3, "The Impact of Private Disinvestment on Workers and Their Communities" and the works cited therein. For a French example, see Centre d'Ethnologie Sociale et de Psycho-Sociologie, *Les Effets Traumatisants d'un Licenciement Collectif* (Paris: CORDES, 1973) and the follow-up by the same institute, *Travail–Classe–Famille: Recherche sur la Vie des Familles Ouvrières à Partir d'un Licenciement Collectif* (Paris: CORDES, 1975). For an international perspective, see Johann Galtung, "Structural Violence," *Journal of Peace Research* (Winter 1976); Charles Mueller, "Migration of the Unemployed: A Relocation Assistance Program," *Monthly Labor Review* (Apr. 1981), pp. 62–64; "Shrinking Families, Economy Dampen American Migration," *Providence Journal*, Feb. 1, 1983, p. X–1; Dominique Motte, "Des processus de licenciement–reclassement comme mécanismes de résistance a la mobilité," in *L'Access aux Emplois et la Mobilité Professionelle* (Paris: Centre d'Etude et de Recherche sur les Qualifications, 1979), pp. 217–39.

10. These conclusions are based on calculations utilizing the statistics found in Bureau of Labor Statistics, *Employment and Earnings, States and Areas, 1939–78* (Washington, D.C.: USGPO, 1979) and Bureau of the Census, *Statistical Abstract of the United States, 1980* (Washington, D.C.: USGPO, 1980). The findings have been confirmed by Dr. Gerald Carlino, senior economist for the Federal Reserve Bank of Philadelphia, quoted in Elizabeth M. Fowler, "Jobs Rising in Rural Sections," *New York Times*, Nov. 11, 1983, p. D27 and John Herbers, "Continuing Growth of Rural Areas Appears Immune to Recession," *New York Times*, Nov. 30, 1982, pp. 1, 16.

11. The calculations are based on statistics from Ministère du Travail, *Tableaux statistiques sur le travail et l'empoi* (Paris: Documentation Française, 1980) and Banque National de Paris, *Guide statistique des 22 régions de France* (Paris: Banque Nationale de Paris, 1979). Confirmation may be found in B. Sinou, "Marseille: Quand on quitte le centre ville," *Sud Information Economique*, no. 47 (3rd qtr., 1981), pp. 19–24 and "Quand la France se compte," *Le Monde*, sélection hebdomadaire, Feb. 16–22, 1984, p. 10, citing the recently published analysis of the 1982 census.

12. For example see, Françoise Stoeckel, "Crise régionale et récomposition de la main d'oeuvre," in *Seminaire d'Économie et de Sociologie du Travail et de la*

Santé (Aix-en-Provence: Laboratoire de l'Economie et de la Sociologie du Travail, 1982); D. Linhart and M. Maruani, "Précarisation et déstabilisation des emplois ouvriers," *Travail et Emploi*, no. 11 (Jan –Mar. 1982); D. Baroin and P. Fracheboud, *Recherches sur les Déterminants de l'Emploi: Le Rôle des PME* (Paris: Travail et Société, 1982); B. Ganne, G. Durel, D. Motte, and H. Puel, *Licenciements Collectifs et Reclassement: Etudes de Cas à Valence* (Lyon: Economie et Humanisme, 1980).

13. Manuel Castells, *The Urban Question* (Cambridge, Mass.: MIT Press, 1980), pp. 462–65; cf. De Gaudemar, *La Mobilisation Générale*, note 9, pp. 218–21.

14. Henry Coing, *L'Entreprise la Ville et le Marche de l'Emploi* (Paris: Doctoral diss. Univ. de Paris V–Sorbonne, 1979), pp. 58–59.

15. The foregoing analysis of the utopian moment is drawn from several sources. The general idea is drawn from Connolly, "Appearance and Reality," *Political Theory*, 7 (Nov. 1969), pp. 445–68; Cf. Aronowitz, *False Promises* (New York: Random House, 1973), note 66, pp. 21–50; David Moberg, "Lordstown Revisited," *In These Times* 8, no. 38 (Oct. 10–16, 1984), pp. 8–9; J.-M. Leduc and P. Rosanvallon, "La nouvelle approche des luttes sur l'emploi," *Analyses* (1974), pp. 4–14; Michèle Bonnechère, "'Protection de l'emploi' et sauvegarde de la 'propriété' capitaliste," *Le Droit Ouvrier*, no. 324 (June 1975), pp. 191–208; D. Gordon, R. Edwards and M. Reich, *Segmented Work, Divided Workers* (Cambridge, Eng.: Cambridge Univ. Press, 1982).

INDEX

INDEX